SUPERBIKE

2003-2004

SUMMARY

GRAPHIC AND PHOTOGRAPHIC DESIGN
STUDIO ZAC!
Fabrizio Porrozzi
Graeme Brown
Alessandro Piredda
Cinzia Giuriolo
Daniela Petrucci

PROJECT AND TEXT
Claudio Porrozzi

Welcome

Dear Friends,

The season that has just concluded has given us some wonderful excitement as the tradition and history of the World Superbike Championship have led us to expect. Many significant changes have characterised this year and the most important was undoubtedly the switch from 750cc to 1000cc four-stroke machines. This change, which was still at an early stage in 2003, will continue to take shape in the 2004 championship, when new teams and bikes are expected to arrive: Honda CBR1000RR, Yamaha R1, Kawasaki ZX10 and, last but not least, the Chinese Zongshen team, the world's number 1 motorcycle manufacturer in terms of numbers. The Endurance racing champions have in fact decided to make their debut in the World Superbike Championship to promote the image of their company. The teams are already hard at work in their efforts to lay down the gauntlet to series dominators Ducati and the increasingly competitive Suzuki and Petronas teams. The vitality of the World Superbike Championship therefore is once again a clear demonstration of the success that has characterised the series since its creation. It has already entered into a new era that will allow it to widen its historic horizons: a great sporting event, a fundamental instrument for the spread of motorcycle racing around the world, and an irreplaceable global shopwindow for production-based motorbikes. Once again the World Superbike Championship, as is its historic tradition, will unite riders, fans from all over the world, sponsors and means of communication in one 'heart', without barriers, to enjoy the same emotions in the name of SPORT. The Fédération Internazionale de Motociclisme and FGSport, who have been united forever, will continue to work together to make what was an American dream in the 1980s become a modern and consolidated reality throughout the world.

Ad majora and here's to the road!

Francesco Zerbi, F.I.M. President

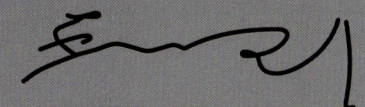

that's su

uperbike

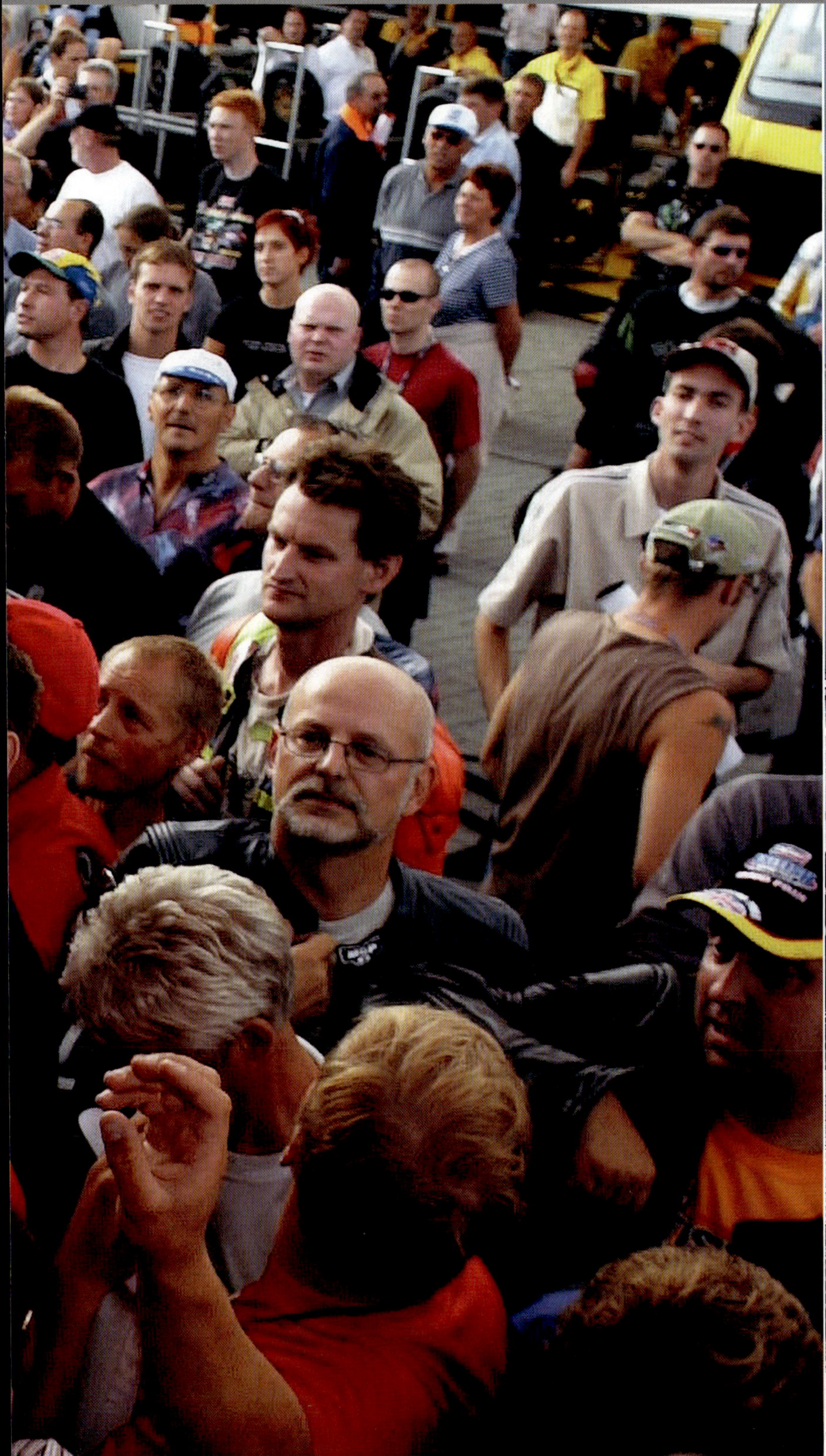

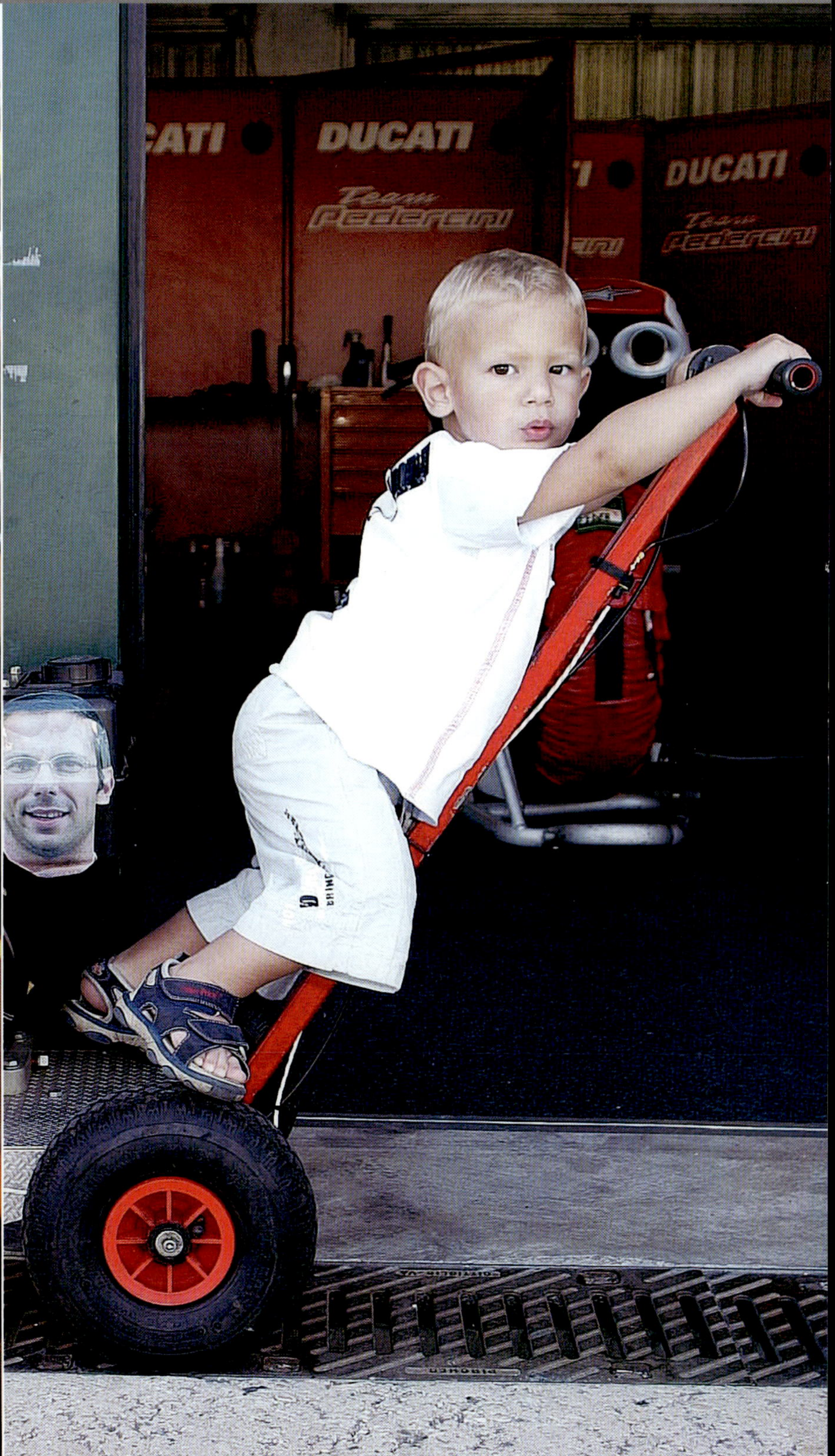

THAT'S SUPERBIKE

After fifteen years it is extremely difficult to give a definition of Superbike because SBK must be experienced in all of its aspects and this is precisely its strength. The racing is quite simply splendid and never monotonous, whether we are talking about the sophisticated (but streetbike-derived) superbikes, the supersports or even the surprising superstocks: and what about the riders, who are the 'stars' both on and off the track, when they appear in the SBK Ring or wander amongst the general public in the paddock? This is the most surprising aspect of Superbike, the fact that it allows the real motorcycle racing fans to come close to the stars of the show: the riders, the bikes and the teams. As we said before, the races are never boring, and they are broadcast throughout the world on global television for the joy of bike fans everywhere; they appreciate every single detail of these standard production run bikes which come from the factory, but which have now reached mon-

THAT'S SUPERBIKE

strous levels of performance. Factory teams and professional outfits help to give Superbike an appearance that is
worthy of the world championship run by FG Sport, which
recently took over from the US giant, Octagon. The Italian
company resumed control of a championship it originally
took over back in 1990, and has launched Superbike onto
the international stage in a period of growth that seems
to go on forever. This combination is an intoxicating one
for all those people who love bikes, and is made up of the
stars of the track and the spectators around the circuit. It
combines the fascination of the two-wheeled sport of ye-
steryear, when catch-fencing and guard-rails did not exist,
with the most advanced technology to be found anywhere
today. But the facts not the words are the most important
thing because Superbike is made to be experienced: only
those people who go to see the races live at the circuits
can really understand what Superbike is all about!

After three disappointing seasons in the mid-1990s on factory Ducati and Kawasaki bikes, few people would have bet on Neil Hodgson becoming a championship winner. Yet the British rider overcame all the sceptics to take the 2003 World Superbike title. The story began on November 20, 1973 when Neil was born in Burnley, Lancashire. His racing career started in 1982 in motocross and Neil soon made a name for himself. After switching to road-racing in 1992, he won the British 125 cc title at his first attempt and then moved into the world category the following year. In 1994 he was snapped up by HRC to ride an RS125: his talent was plain for all to see and before the end of the season he switched to the Yamaha Harris team in the 500 cc class and then to WCM with a ROC-Yamaha, earning the title of rookie of the year. "I was actually quite a good two-stroke rider" he says. "In 1995 I was the best privateer in my first season, I was just 21 years old and had a rosy future ahead of me". Neil then made a risky decision to accept an offer from Ducati to race with the 1996 World Superbike factory team alongside Troy Corser. The expected results failed to come, Neil finished tenth overall, but the Bologna-based team confirmed him for the following season, when he finished ninth. Released from his contract at the end of 1997, Hodgson switched to Kawasaki, but could only manage eleventh overall. At this point he teamed up with GSE Racing and decided to return to the domestic championship. In his second season in British Superbikes, Neil won

NEIL HODGSON

the title after a superb battle with Chris Walker (Suzuki). But more important was the fact that he won two rounds of the World Superbike Championship, demonstrating that he had reached a mature competitive level. In 2001, Neil returned to the World Superbike championship with GSE Racing and finished fifth overall in his debut season. His best performances were his win at Donington, his record lap at Misano, numerous podiums and pole positions. 2002 saw another superb season for Neil with the same team and in the same championship, and he finished third overall. These results guaranteed him a place as factory rider in the Ducati Fila team for 2003. This season looked to be an easy one only on paper. Living up to the Ducati reputation of titles and record-breaking wins compensated for the lack of any real opposition (with the exception of team-mate Ruben Xaus and Suzuki's Gregorio Lavilla). Hodgson basically had a lot to lose... "I worked hard all year" he adds. "At the start of the season I was a bit worried about switching tyres from Dunlop to Michelin, but I soon got used to

them. I was sure that this was going to be my year, especially as I had the best bike and the best tyres. That's what it's been like all year. Everything was going perfect until Misano when I lost 30 points in one weekend. It changed my mentality and I rode defensively instead of attacking, which is a shame, but there again you win a championship with consistency". In the end Neil won the title with a large points margin to spare over his rivals, who were ready and waiting to take advantage of the rare mistakes of the new world champion. "Winning the 2003 World Superbike Championship with Ducati Fila is a dream come true, the reward for 20 years' hard work" was how Neil summed up the title he won at Assen two rounds before the end of the championship. His sincere words symbolize the good-natured and friendly character of this British rider, who turns into a true fighter when the lights go green. Neil lives on the Isle of Man with his wife Kathryn, who gave birth to their first daughter, Holly Jean, just a few days before his Assen triumph.

NEIL HODGSON

RUBEN XAUS

ruben

RUBEN XAUS

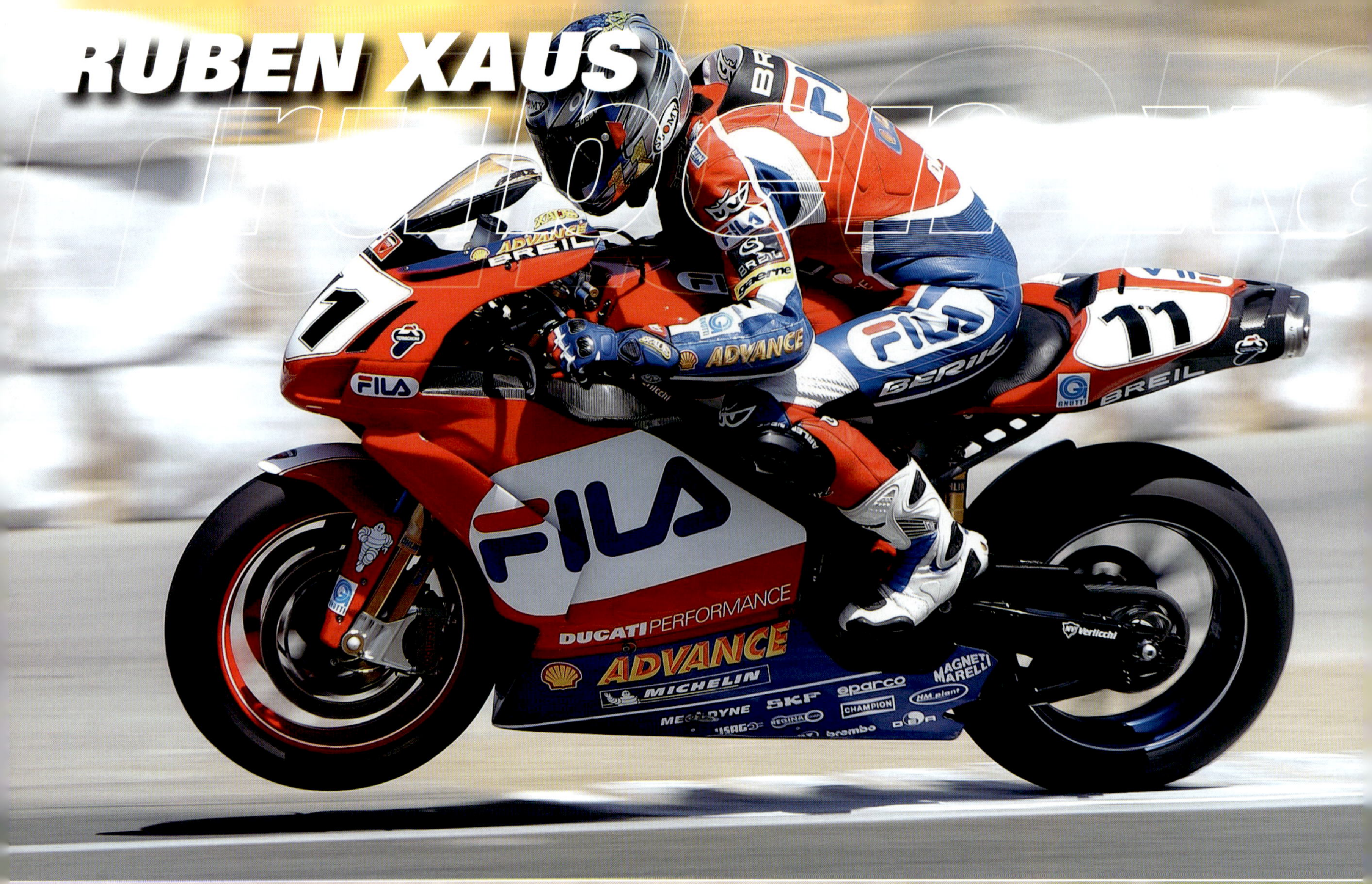
FILA
11
DUCATI PERFORMANCE
ADVANCE
MICHELIN
BREIL
SKF
CHAMPION
MAGNETI MARELLI
brembo

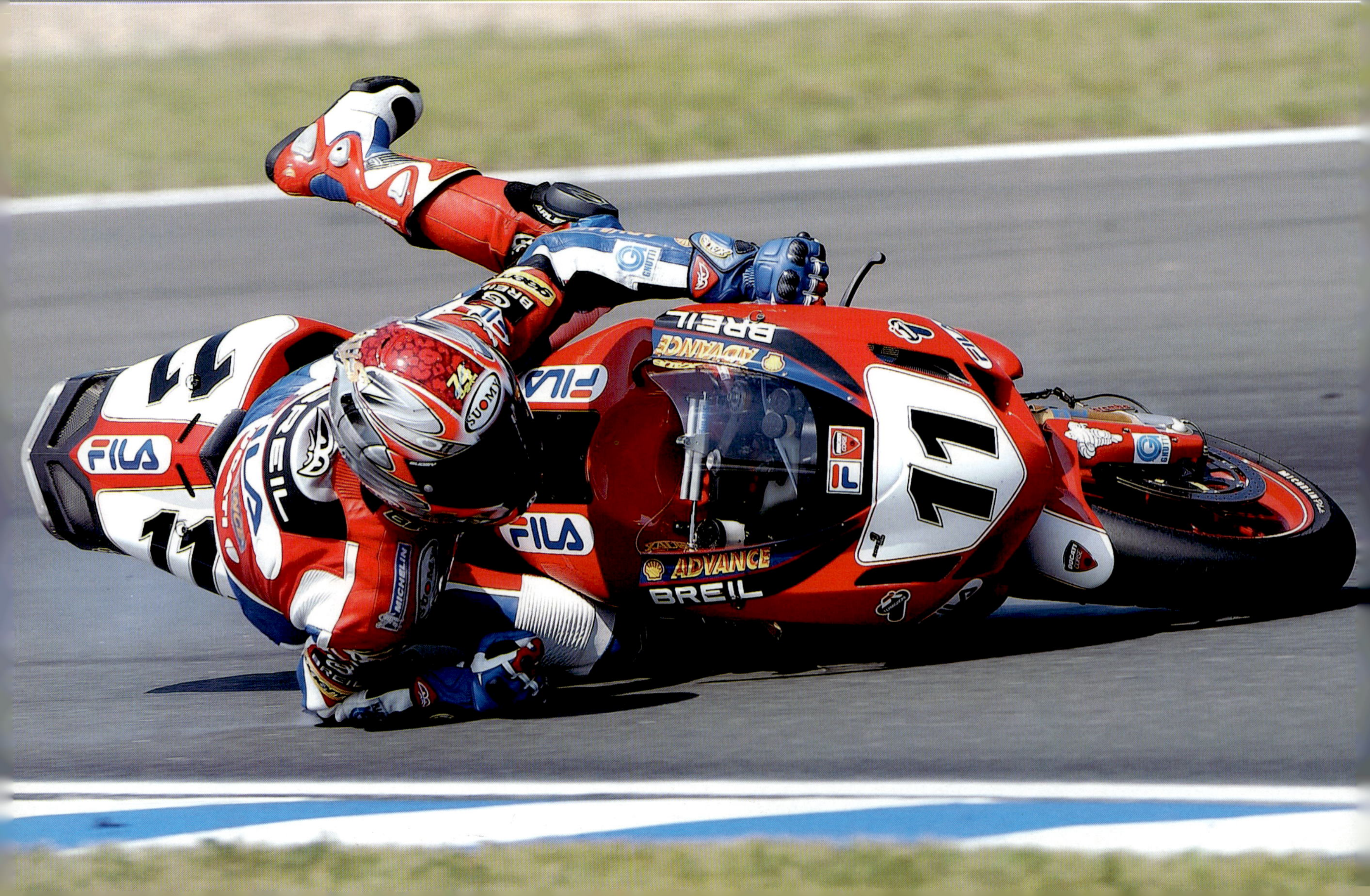
BREIL
ADVANCE
FILA
11

to Thunderbike, before returning to the supersport category. In 2000 he arrived in Ducati, who gave him a slot in the factory Supersport team, and he finished seventh overall. His results were so impressive that the following year he was promoted to Superbike by the Borgo Panigale factory, winning his first race at Oschersleben. He was rightly confirmed for the 2002 season, but despite the high expectations, he could only finish sixth, the same result as the previous year. Ruben in fact alternated some superb performances with spectacular crashes and a reckless ri-

ding style. This year the Catalan rider began well, but Japan saw the start of a disappointing run of form until Misano where he scored a double victory and the first of his seven wins this year. Unfortunately his return to form began a bit late, otherwise the championship race would for sure have been different. Ruben is an extremely quick and talented rider but is still very reckless: he could easily be the man to beat in Superbike, but often his results are studded with crashes and falls that often deprive him of the points required to be a contender for the title.

RUBEN XAUS

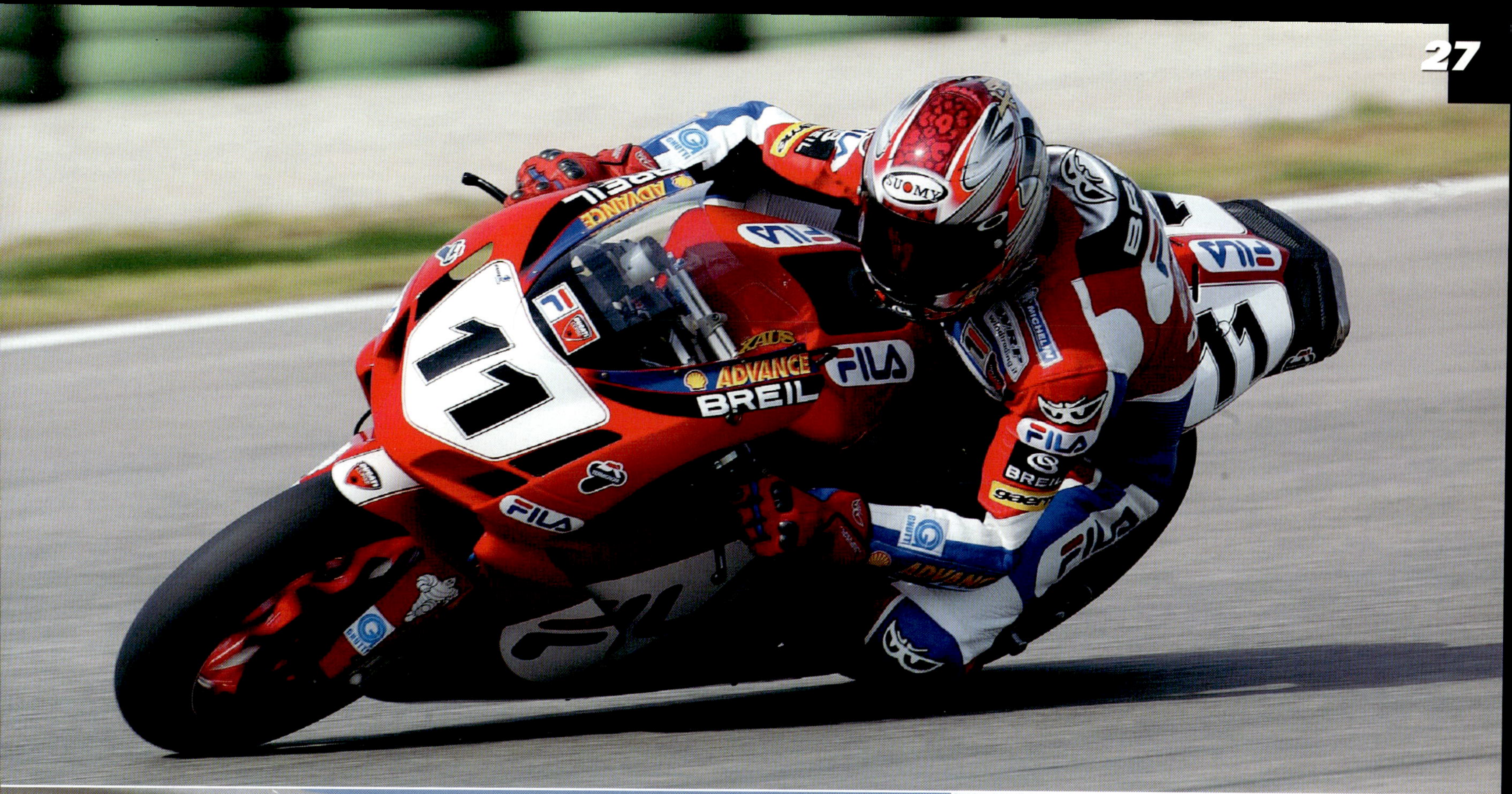
11
ADVANCE
BREIL
FILA

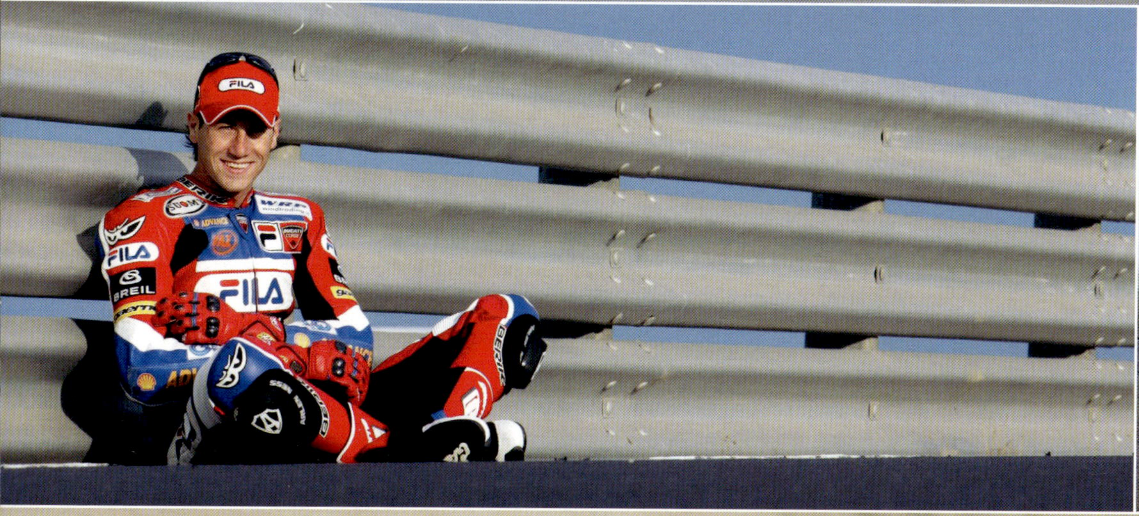
FILA

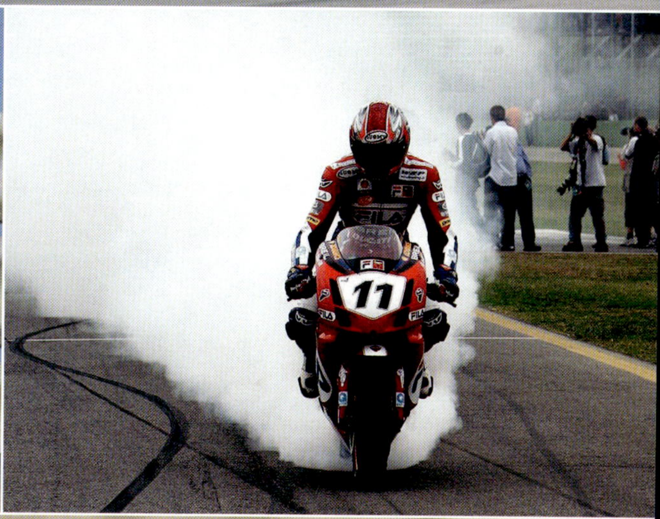
11

FILA
DUCATI PERFORMANCE
ADVANCE
MICHELIN
SKF
MEGADYNE

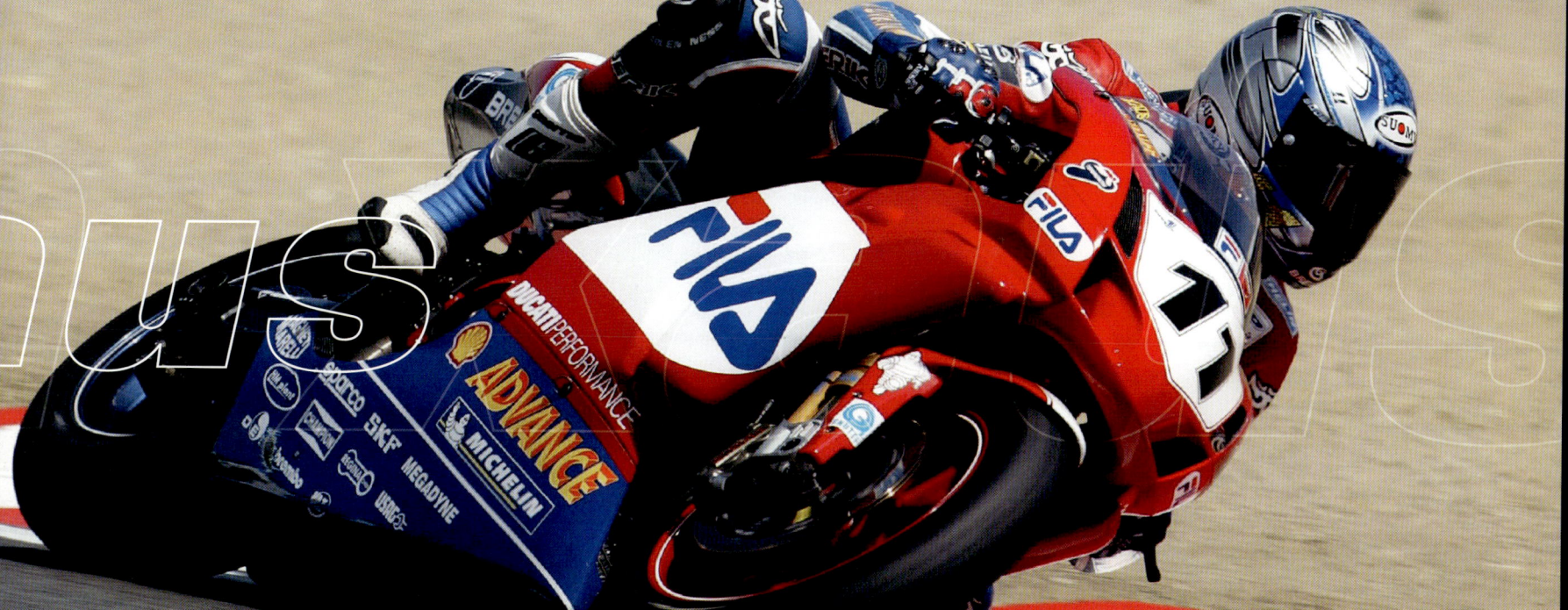

suzuki

000 GSX-R

SUZUKI GSX-R 1000

S uzuki are one of the teams with the biggest image in Superbike and one of the most qualified, even though the last few seasons have been slightly disappointing, but this can certainly not be put down to its riders or management. Until 2002 Alstare Corona had to count on the 'old' and no longer competitive Suzuki GSX-R 750; this year however expectations were high with the promising GSX-R 1000. Suzuki were the first manufacturer to accept the '1000cc four-cylinder' challenge, and worked wonders to get the new bike to the track in

January in Malaysia with Gregorio Lavilla. The Spanish rider, born on September 29, 1973 at Hospitalet de Infant, had previously raced with a private Ducati and a factory Kawasaki; in 2002 he switched to Alstare Corona Suzuki. Lavilla is a pleasant guy and until the arrival of Ruben Xaus in 2001, he had long been the favourite of the Spanish public. Singleton rider for the Japanese manufacturer, Gregorio took it upon himself to see to the development of the new bike which virtually took place race by race. The first part of the season saw a

GSX-R 100

massive improvement and at Sugo, Monza and Silverstone the Suzuki finished right behind Hodgson's Ducati, giving the impression that a win was on the cards. However despite some good results in the second half of the season (including two more podiums), this positive trend went unconfirmed. Suzuki finished second overall in the final standings and Lavilla fifth, but the impression is that the results could have been much better had Suzuki put more effort into the project. In fact, judging by the times obtained by their superstock bikes, the Japanese four-cylinder machines, which are reckoned to have more than 200 HP, could have been real front-runners, as demonstrated by the title wins in national championships throughout the world. On several occasions, Lavilla was flanked by Vittorio Iannuzzo, who had the support of Suzuki Italia and Team Alstare. The bike of the 21 year-old rider from Avellino, Italy was not a factory machine but it enabled the former European Superstock champion to occasionally make a name for himself, in particular with a front-row start at Misano.

SUZUKI GSX-R 1000

SUZUKI GSX-R 1000

Suzuki GSX-R 1000

Engine
Type: **four-cylinder inline**
Displacement: **998 cc**
Bore x stroke: **73 x 59 mm**
Valves: **four per cylinder**
Power: **185 HP @ 13.500 rpm**

Chassis/Suspension
Frame: **aluminium twin-spar**
Front suspension: **upside-down forks**
Rear suspension: **single shock absorber**

Transmission
Gearbox: **six-speed**
Clutch: **dry**

Brakes
Make: **Brembo**
Front: **2 x 320 mm discs**
Rear: **1 x 220 mm disc**

Tyres
Make: **Dunlop**
Front: **120/80ZR 16.5**
Rear: **180/75ZR 16.5**

Dimensions
Length: **2.045 mm**
Width: **715 mm**
Dry weight: **167 kg**
Wheelbase: **1.410 mm**
Fuel tank: **18 litres**

s winners

DUCATI WINNERS

In 2003 the big question mark surrounding Superbike was whether or not the 999 could inherit the successful mantle left by the 998 (and the 996 and 916 before it). Just to be on the safe side however, the evolution of the previous all-conquering model continued. The factory bikes from the 2003 season, the 998 F02, were handed over to the HM Plant-GSE team which entered youngster James Toseland and expert Chris Walker. It was the 23 year-old from Doncaster who took the win at Oschersleben in race 2 to send the British fans wild. To-

seland, who arrived in four-stroke racing in 1998 with supersport, switched to Superbike in 2001 and scored some good results up to his win this year. In 2004 he has been snapped up by the factory Ducati squad. Another win for an 'old' Ducati, this time a 998 RS 02, was obtained by Pierfrancesco Chili at the legendary Laguna Seca track in California. The 39 year-old Bologna rider, who has always been one of the stars of Superbike, this year began a new adventure with the small but efficient PSG-1 outfit. Chili has always been one of the top finishers in World Super-

HM plant
HITACHI
CONSTRUCTION EQUIPMENT
DUNLOP
DUCATI

DUNLOP
HM plant
HITACHI
GSE RACING

HM plant
52

HM plant
HITACHI
GSE RACING
DUNLOP
52
inners

DUCATI WINNERS

DUCATI WINNERS

bike and he stepped up to the podium eight times, finishing seventh overall, a result that will allow 'Frankie' to keep his favourite number 7 on the bike for next year. While a win was expected from Toseland and above all Chili, the real surprise came from another British rider, Shane Byrne on the MonsterMob Ducati 998, who scored a totally unexpected double win at Brands Hatch. At the age of 26, Byrne's splendid year was completed with the British Superbike title.

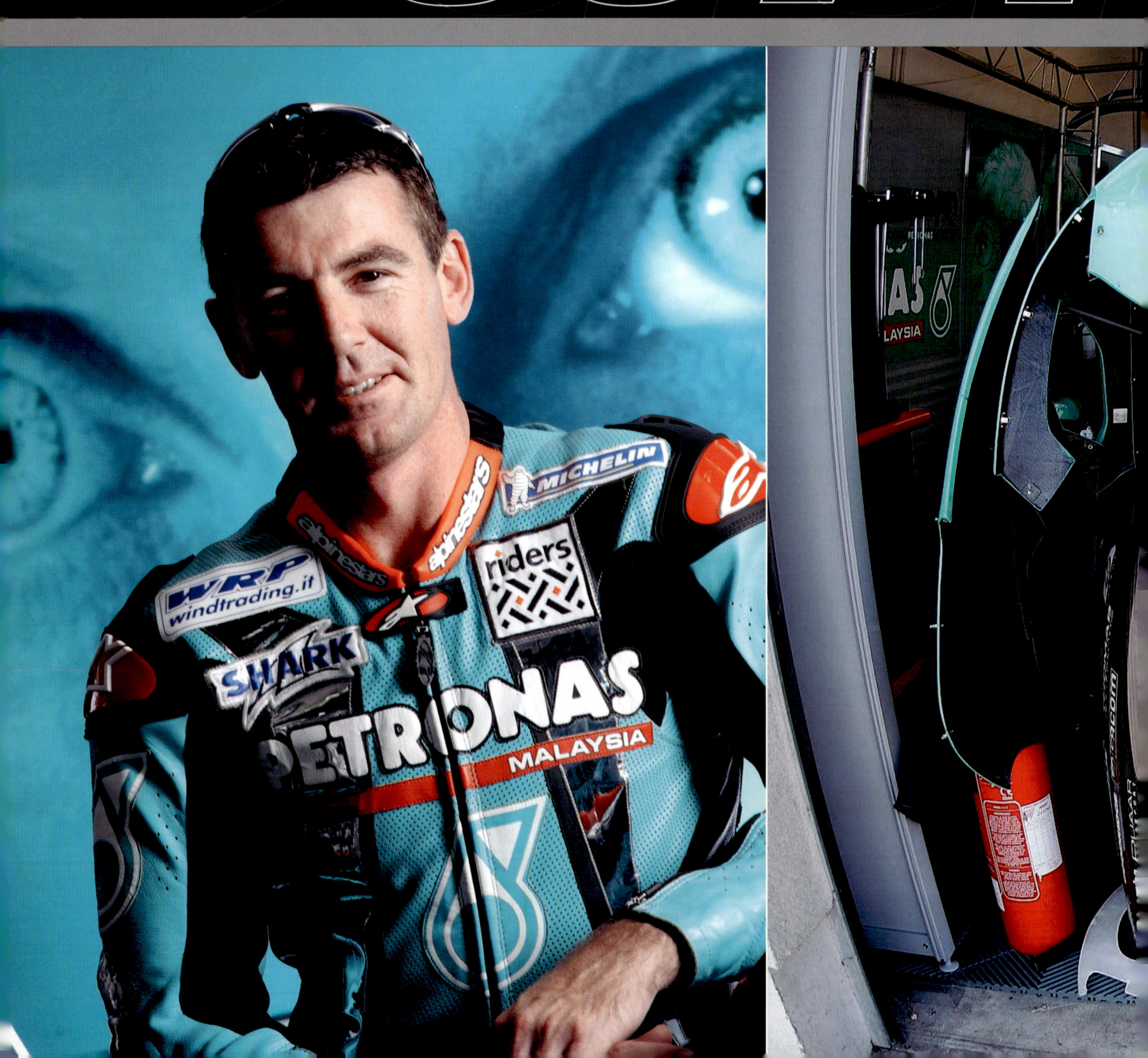

as

petronas

FOGGY PETRONAS

Not many people would have put their gambling money on the project set up by the Malaysian national oil company. The names Carl Fogarty and Troy Corser gave the impression that the venture was a serious one, but the continuous delays in the MotoGP debut and its eventually resorting to entry into World Superbike did not help much. Nevertheless the Foggy Petronas FP1 made it to the grid for its debut at the opening round of the 2003 World Superbike championship in Valencia. The riders were Corser and 30 year-old Brit James Haydon. The 900 cc three-cylinder bike had a declared power output of 185 HP, but the development work carried out by the team run by Carl and Michaela Fogarty soon ran into a number of problems with its Suter-designed engines. The triple made a sensational sight as it shot flames from the exhausts under braking, which caused a few problems for chasing riders! Once FIM homologation had been obtained, Petronas took part in the world cham-

pionship but failed to obtain any major results. In the second half of the season however, the former Aprilia/Ducati rider and 1996 world champion Troy Corser did manage to obtain some improvements from the bike to move up the results sheets. His team-mate was not so impressive and despite having a certain experience in WSBK (he made his debut in 1997), Haydon only managed to score points three times in 24 races. The Australian never gave in, trying to gain as much experience as possible and pick up points here and there. Twelfth overall in the final standings was clearly not satisfactory for a rider of his calibre, but it is not a bad result if we consider that the Anglo-Malaysian bike had made its first shakedown run on a German circuit in October 2002. The best result for the FP1 (which finished just a few points behind Kawasaki in the final standings) was fifth place at Phillip Island, followed by a sixth place at Assen, again in the hands of Corser.

FOGGY PETRONAS

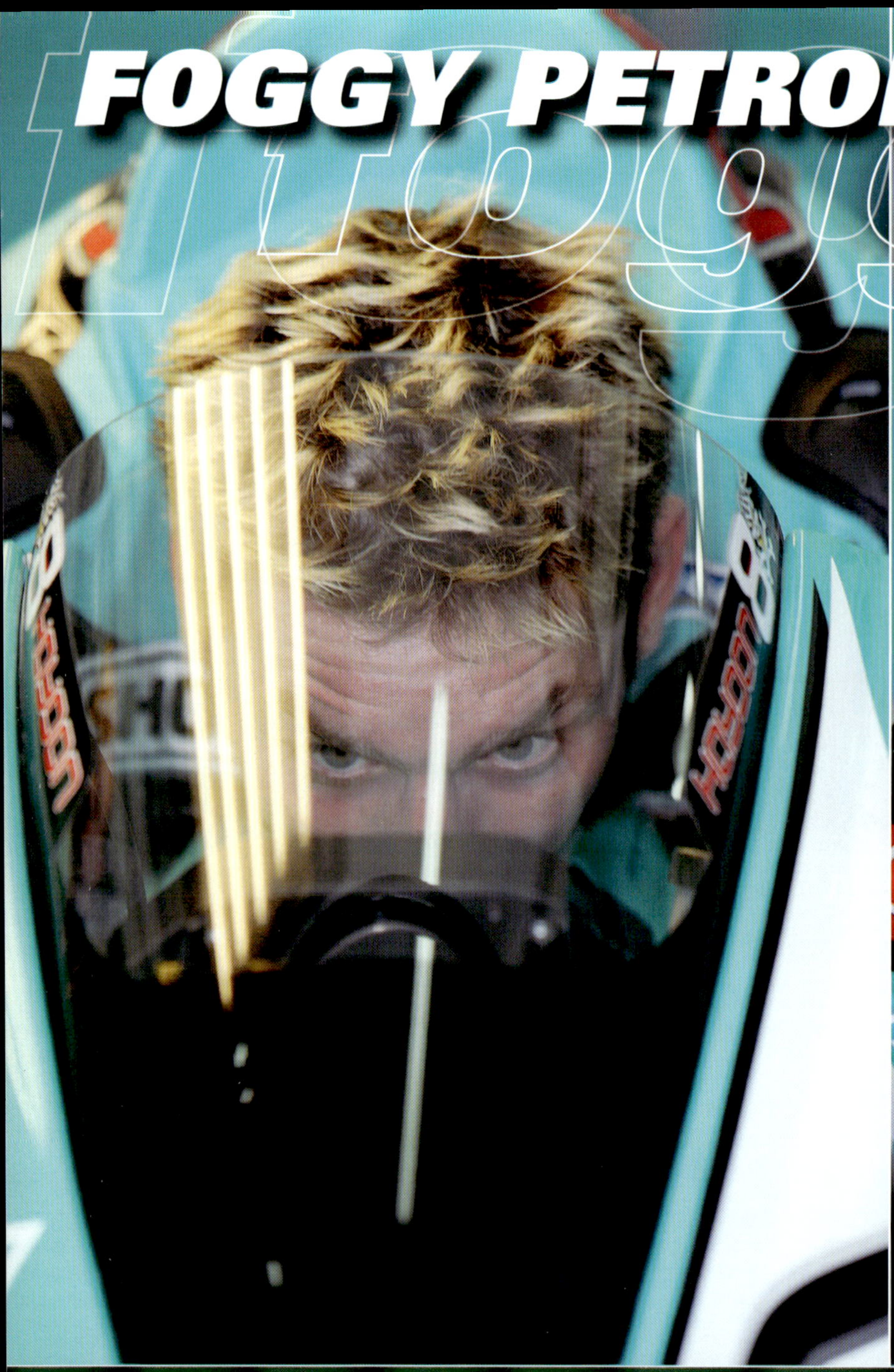

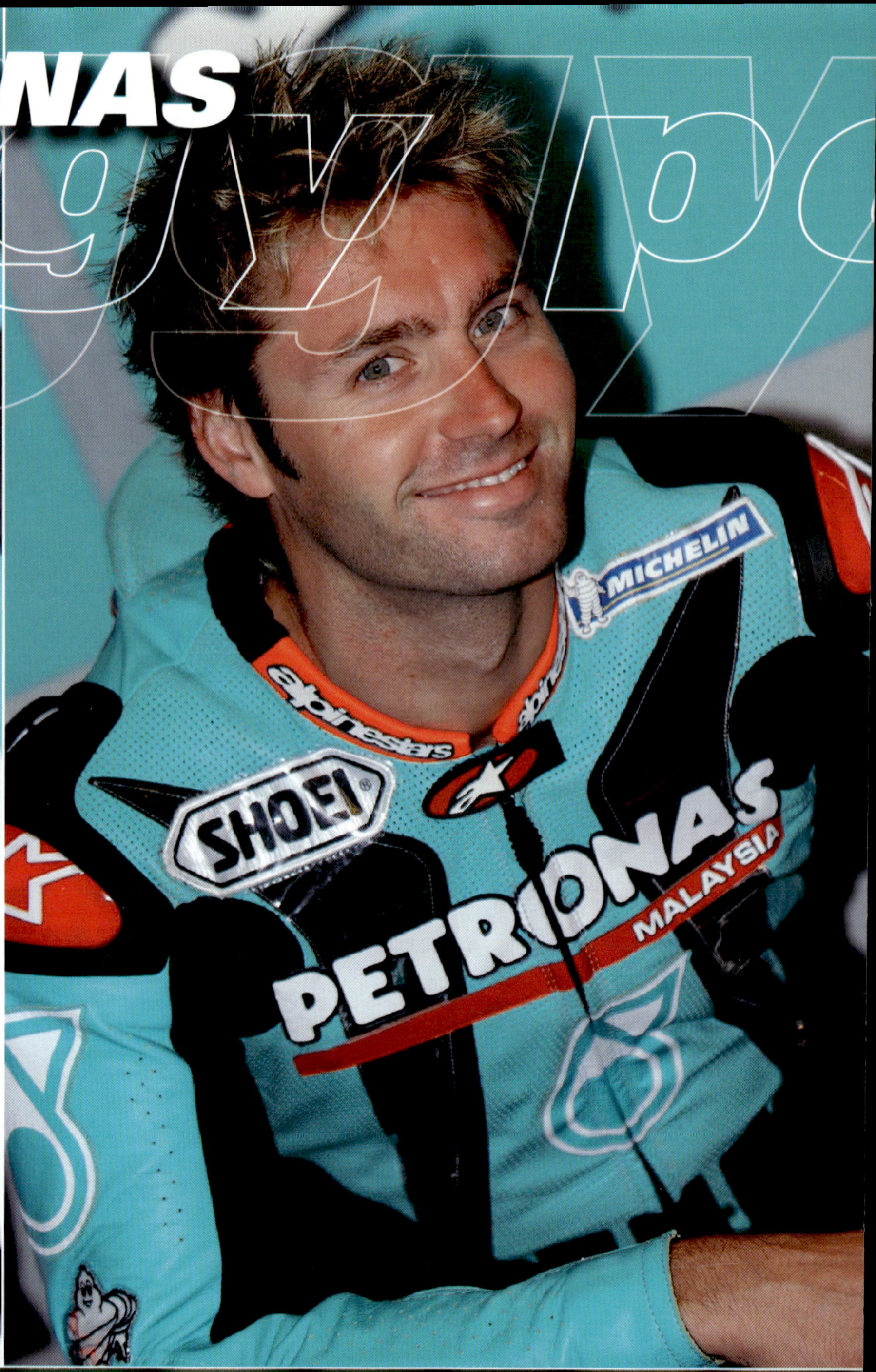

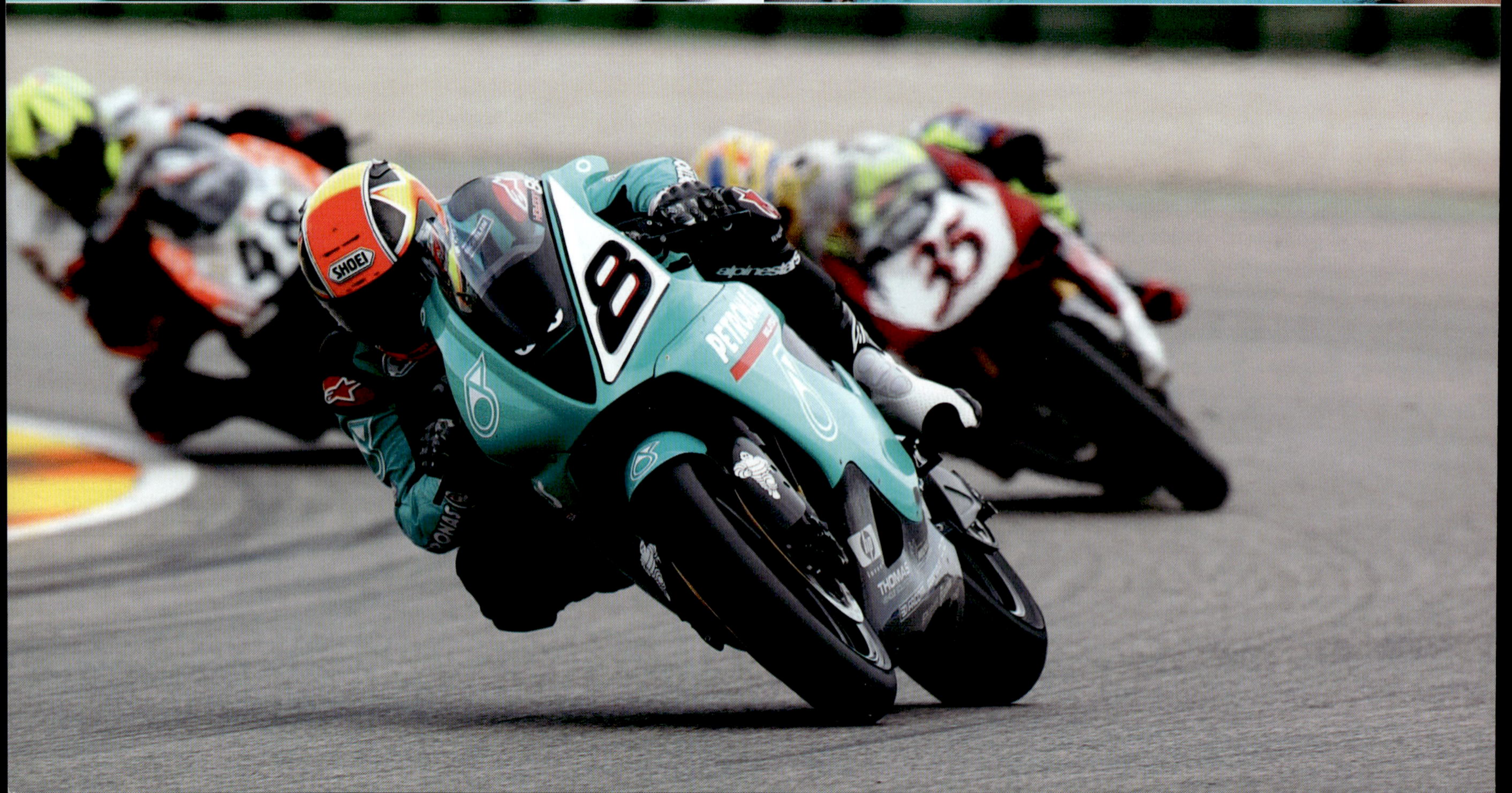

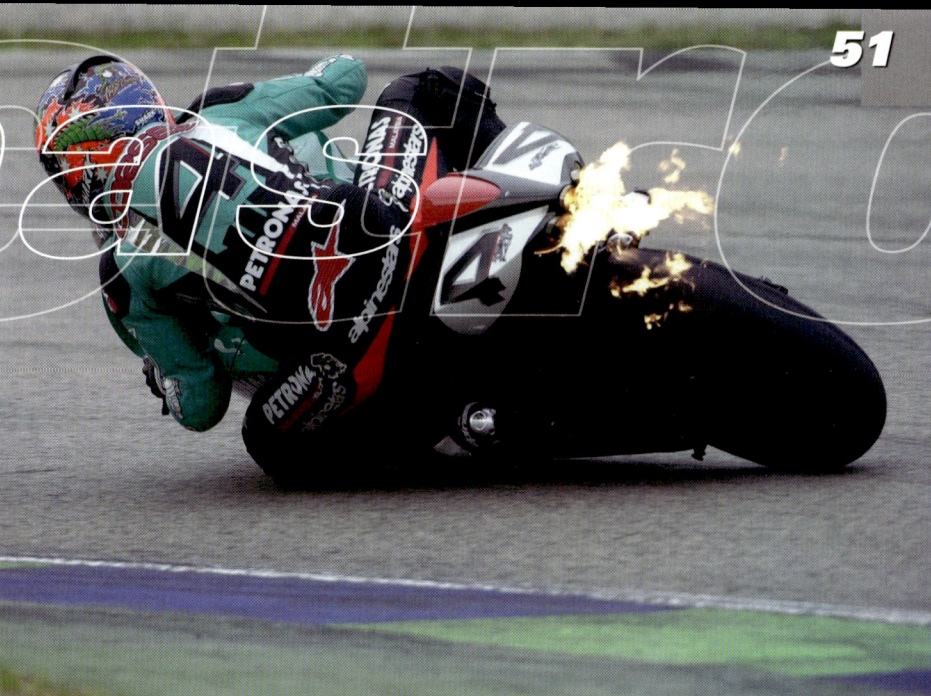

Petronas Foggy FP1

Engine
Type: **three-cylinder inline**
Displacement: **899.5 cc**
Bore x stroke: **88 x 49,3 mm**
Valves: **four per cylinder**
Power: **185 HP @ 13.500 rpm**

Chassis/Suspension
Front suspension: **Öhlins forks**
Rear suspension: **Öhlins single shock**

Transmission
Gearbox: **six-speed**
Clutch: **dry**

Brakes
Make: **Brembo**
Front: **2 x 320 mm**
Rear: **220 mm**

Tyres
Make: **Michelin**
Front: **3.50 x 16.5**
Rear: **6.00 x 16.5**

Dimensions
Length: **2.045 mm**
Width: **680 mm**
Dry weight: **162 kg**
Wheelbase: **1.425 mm**
Fuel tank: **23.5 litres**

DUCATI RIDERS

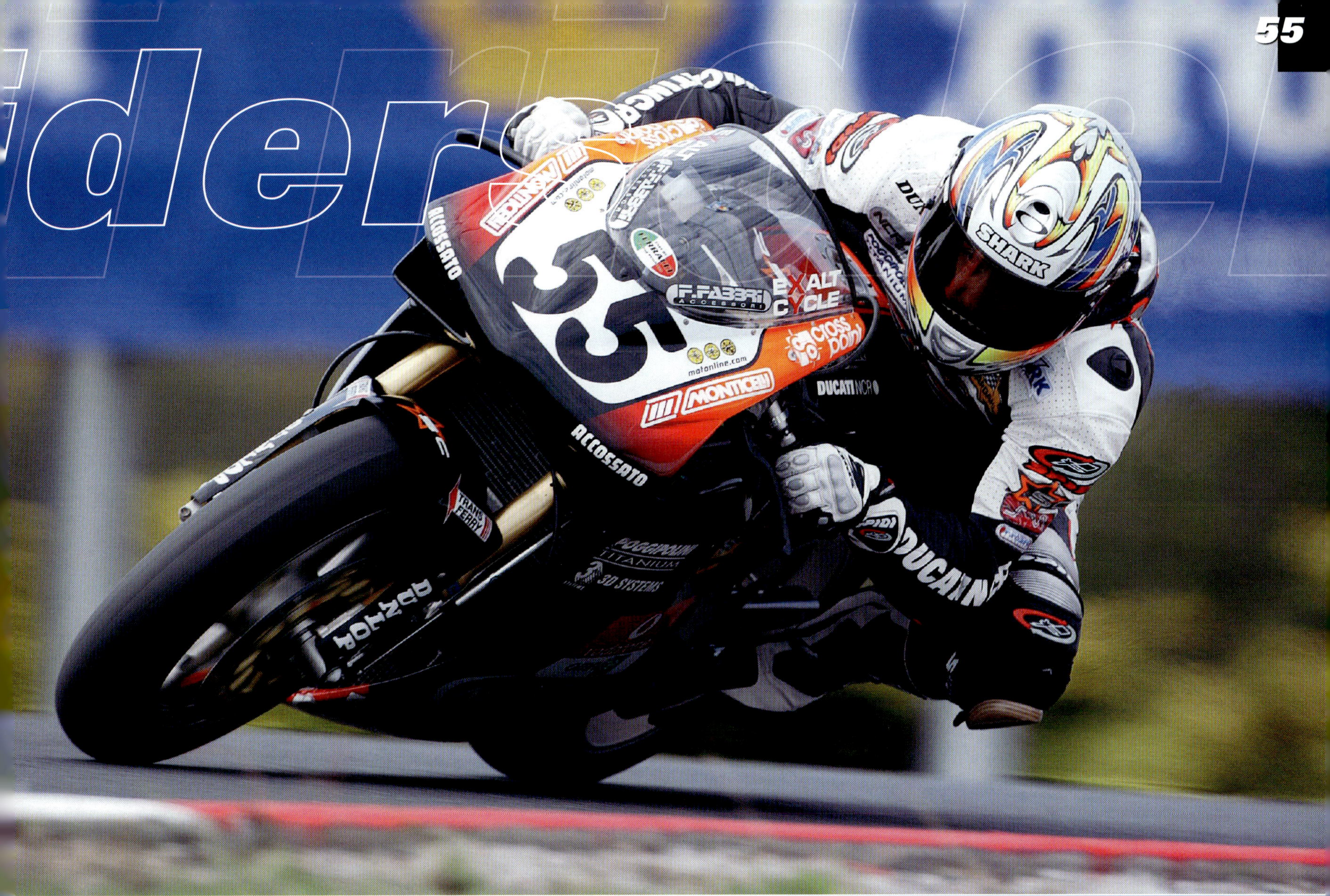
SHARK
F.FABBRI
EXALT CYCLE
MONTIORI
ACCOSSATO
DUCATI CORSE
3D SYSTEMS

RBIKE
MPIONSHIP
MB 2003
www.regisl aconi.com
FGS
worldsbk
GSP

48
vodafone
ACCOSSATO

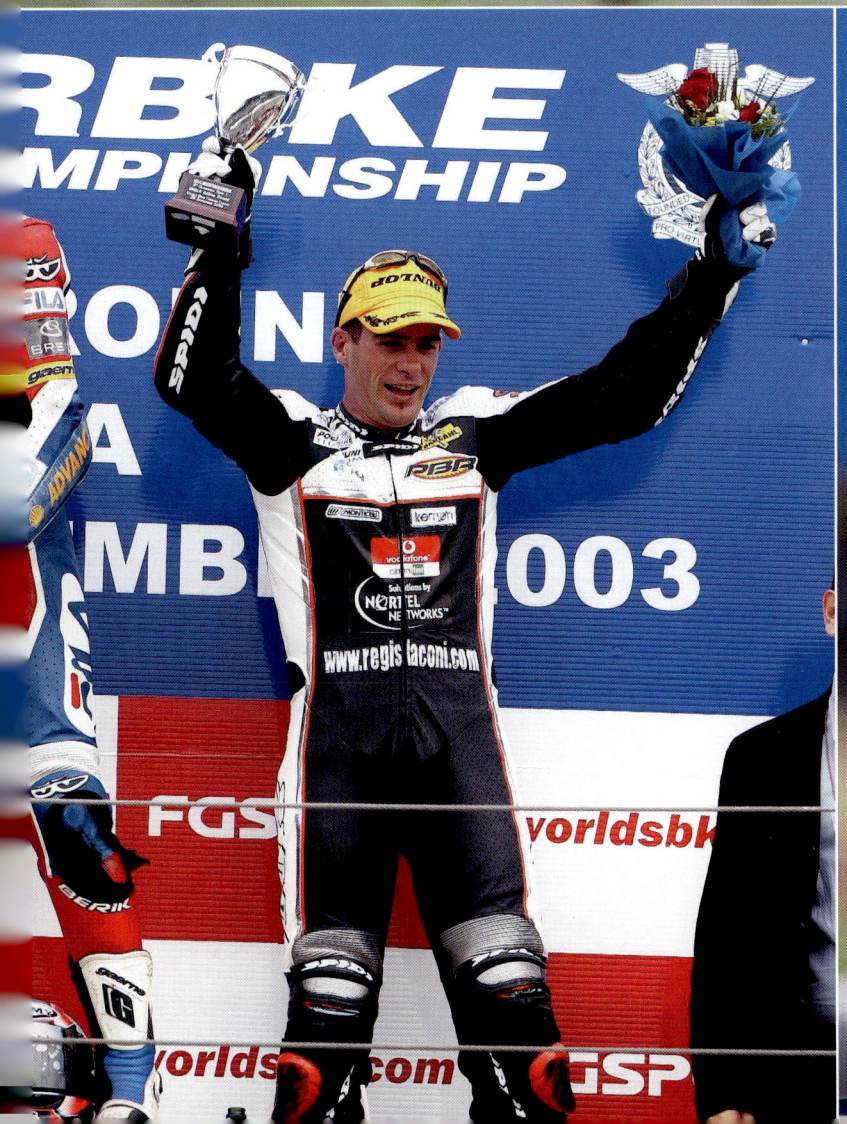

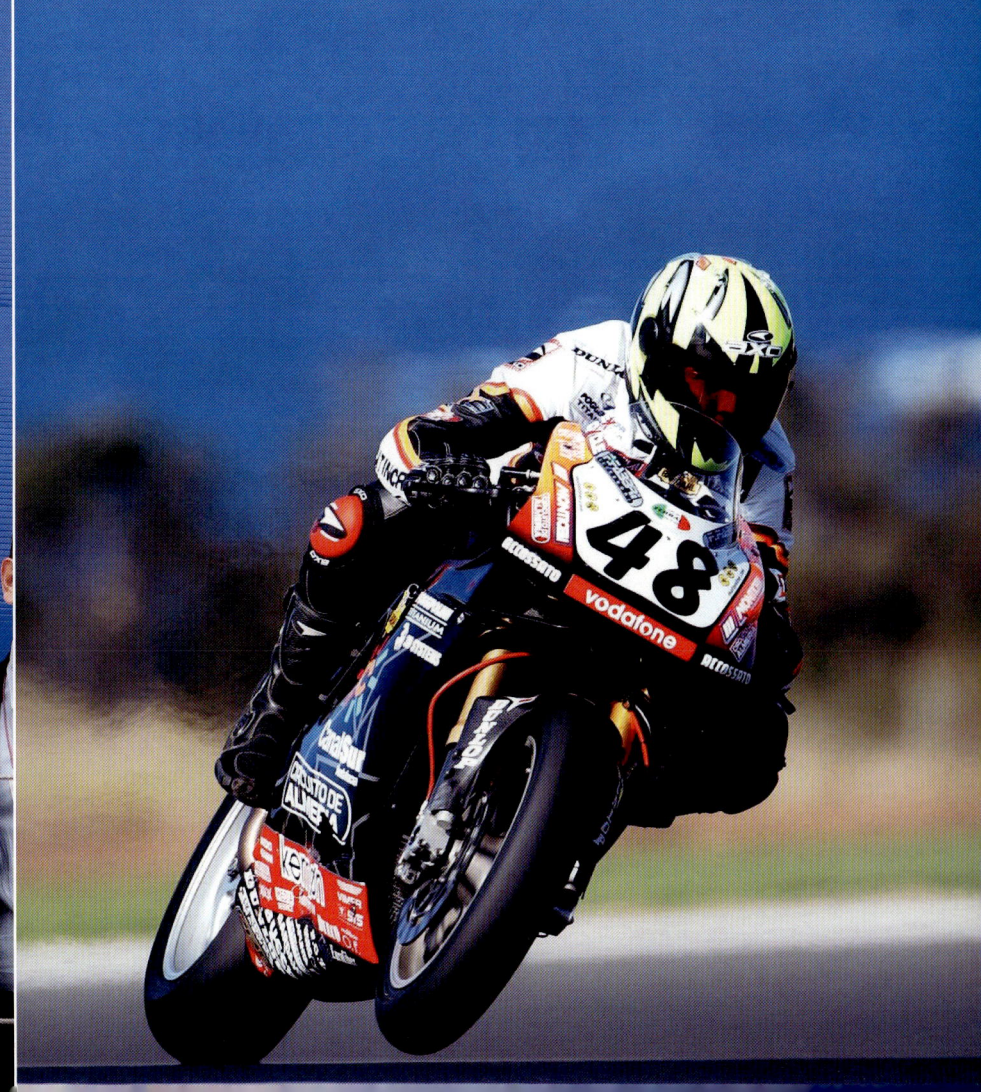

Ducati does not just mean the team Fila 999 and the victorious 998 however, but also the other 998s which the remaining riders used to score precious championship points. Some top names were amongst the list, including Laconi, Walker and Martin. The biggest name was undoubtedly that of Regis Laconi, who raced a 998 RS 03 for the Caracchi NCR team. After making his Superbike debut in 2001, Regis switched to MotoGP for one year but then came back to WSBK in 2003. The 28 year-old Frenchman

DUCATI RIDERS

has one win to his credit, but he should be able to express his true potential in 2004 when he forms part of the factory Ducati team. Thirty-one year-old Brit Chris Walker, the other rider for the HM Plant-GSE team, has considerable experience and he often finished on the podium with an ex-factory 998 F02. Chris finished sixth overall, his best Superbike championship result since his debut in 1997. Another 998 RS 03 allowed Lucio Pedercini, the former 500GP rider, to finish ninth overall. The Mantua-born

Italian had a series of constant results and without some technical problems (and a few crashes) he would surely have finished further up the table. Two other Ducati riders finished in the top 10 in this year's championship: Steve Martin and Marco Borciani, who are linked by an interesting fact. As well as racing in the same team, DFX Ducati, together with Spaniard Borja, they were the riders who experimented with the Pirelli tyres that will be used by all participants in the 2003 championship. Australian Steve

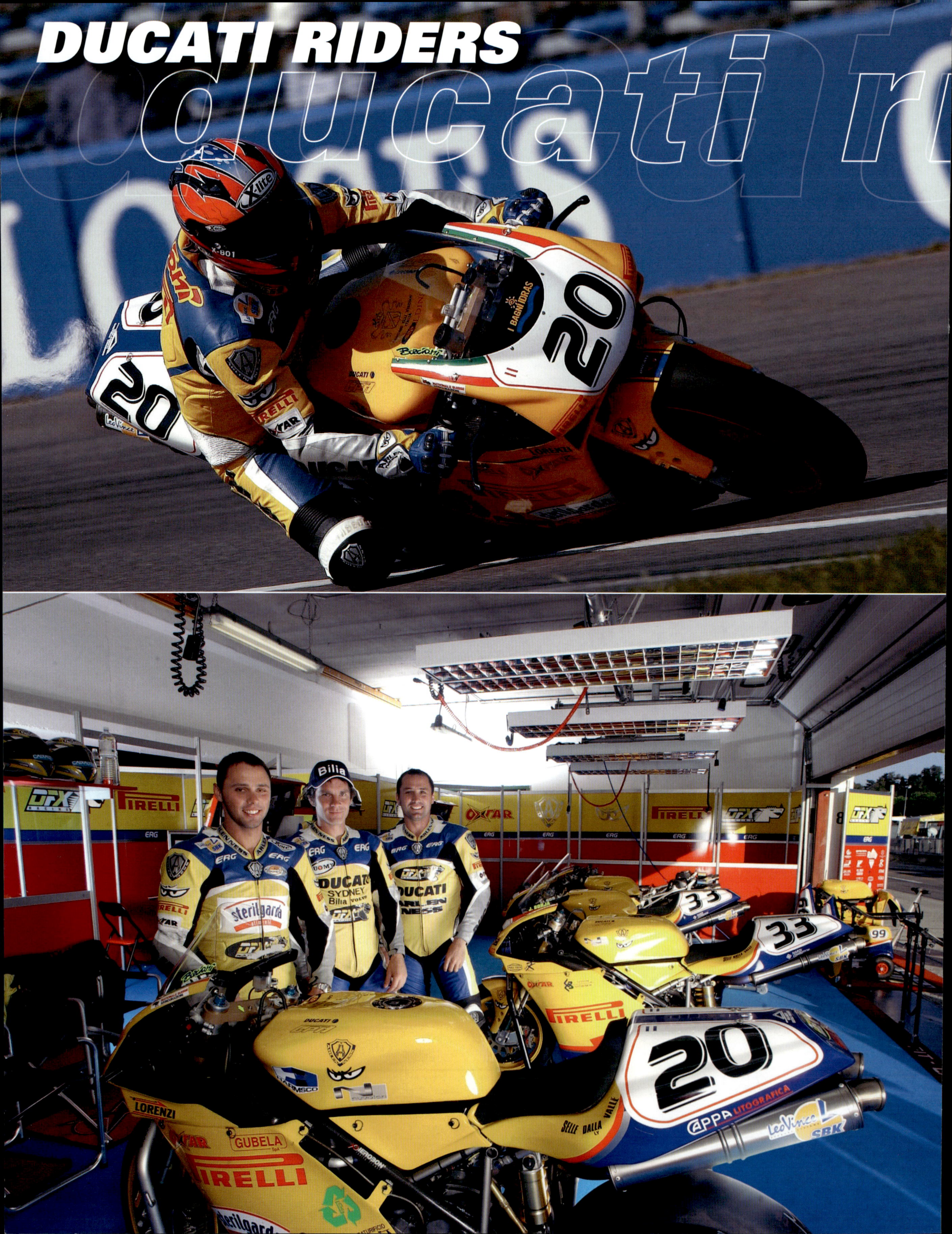

Martin (born in Chastone on December 2, 1968) made his debut in 1997 in Superbike and has raced with a Ducati for the past three years. In 2003 with the 998 RS 03 he finished eighth overall with some up-and-down performances. Marco Borciani didn't really stand out in 2003 but finished tenth overall with some regular performances. In Superbike since 2000, the Italian rider from the province of Brescia has always ridden a Ducati, and this tradition continued in 2003 when he got his hands on a 998 RS 02.

RR
ki ZX7R

KAWASAKI ZX7RR

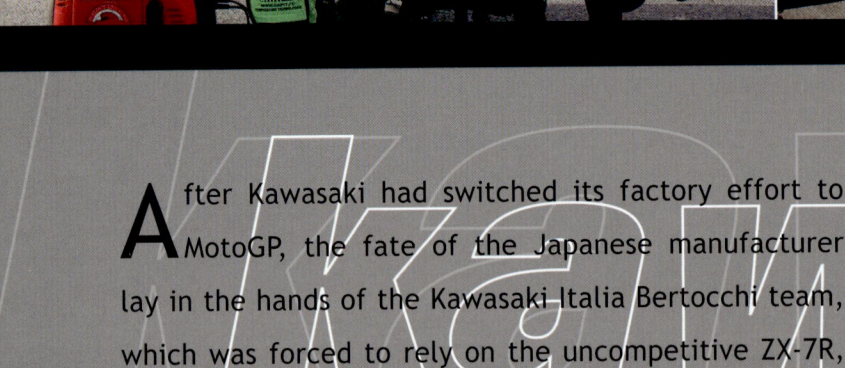

After Kawasaki had switched its factory effort to MotoGP, the fate of the Japanese manufacturer lay in the hands of the Kawasaki Italia Bertocchi team, which was forced to rely on the uncompetitive ZX-7R, the last remaining 750cc machine on the grid.

The four-cylinder Kawasaki gave away 250cc to the 1000cc Ducati machines, with the same weight. As it only had ex-factory material, the Trieste-based team could only hope for reliability to play a hand in allowing Mauro Sanchini and Ivan Clementi to score points. The best result however was a seventh place for Clementi at Assen. After a 2002 season which had led the team to hope for a few top 10 positions, this year highlighted the overwhelming gap between the 750 cc bikes and the 1000 cc machines. Things should improve in 2004 when the ZX-10R is scheduled to make its debut.

Eleventh overall was the best result obtained so far by 33 year-old Mauro Sanchini from Pesaro after the Ita-

lian, who started racing late in life, soon made up the experience gap from the top riders.

28 year-old Ivan Clementi from Montegiorgio in the province of Ascoli Piceno, came to Superbike from 125s and soon proved his talent, finishing fourteenth overall in the final standings.

KAWASAKI ZX7RR

ZXRR

MALOSSI
99

SUPERPOLE
Corona Extra
AXO
BREIL
worldsbk.com

DUNLOP
ARROW
MOTO CLUB MISANO
bitubo
Kawasaki
PNEUS CAR
TAURUS

Classifica Superbike

1	N. Hodgson	(GBR)	Ducati	489
2	R. Xaus	(ESP)	Ducati	386
3	J. Toseland	(GBR)	Ducati	271
4	R. Laconi	(FRA)	Ducati	267
5	G. Lavilla	(ESP)	Suzuki	256
6	C. Walker	(GBR)	Ducati	234
7	P. Chili	(ITA)	Ducati	197
8	S. Martin	(AUS)	Ducati	139
9	L. Pedercini	(ITA)	Ducati	112
10	M. Borciani	(ITA)	Ducati	111
11	M. Sanchini	(ITA)	Kawasaki	108
12	T. Corser	(AUS)	Petronas	107
13	J. Borja	(ESP)	Ducati	87
14	I. Clementi	(ITA)	Kawasaki	76
15	G. Bussei	(ITA)	Yamaha	52
16	S. Byrne	(GBR)	Ducati	50
17	J. Reynolds	(GBR)	Suzuki	42
18	V. Iannuzzo	(ITA)	Suzuki	37
19	A. Gramigni	(ITA)	Yamaha	37
20	Y. Kagayama	(JPN)	Suzuki	35
21	L. Haslam	(GBR)	Ducati	35
22	D. Garcia	(ESP)	Ducati	28
23	M. Rutter	(GBR)	Ducati	23
24	H. Izutsu	(JPN)	Honda	20
25	M. Mladin	(AUS)	Suzuki	13
26	J. Haydon	(GBR)	Petronas	12
27	S. Fuertes	(ESP)	Suzuki	12
28	S. Emmet	(GBR)	Ducati	11
29	N. Russo	(ITA)	Ducati	11
30	A. Yates	(USA)	Suzuki	10
31	D. Ellison	(GBR)	Ducati	9
32	S. Gimbert	(FRA)	Suzuki	8
33	A. Watanabe	(JPN)	Suzuki	8
34	S. Foti	(ITA)	Ducati	8
35	W. Tortoroglio	(ITA)	Honda	6
36	B. Stey	(FRA)	Honda	6
37	H. Saiger	(AUT)	Yamaha	6
38	C. Zaiser	(AUT)	Suzuki	4
39	K. Nakamura	(JPN)	Honda	4
40	L. Pedersoli	(ITA)	Ducati	3
41	P. Blora	(ITA)	Ducati	3
42	F. Protat	(FRA)	Yamaha	3
43	G. Liverani	(ITA)	Yamaha	2
44	L. Pini	(ITA)	Suzuki	2
45	J.Mrkyvka	(CZE)	Ducati	2

RACES Valencia (ESP) • 02/03/03

The 2003 championship got underway at Valencia with the debut of the Anglo-Malaysian Petronas bike, which although not expected to offer much opposition to Ducati, was followed with close interest by everyone in the WSBK paddock. In qualifying Hodgson soon showed he meant business and he was followed by Toseland, Xaus and a surprisingly competitive Corser on the Petronas, while Lavilla with the new Suzuki was only twelfth. Toseland made the initial attack but the factory Ducatis and Walker soon passed him. Hodgson and Xaus repeated the 1-2 in the second race while this time Toseland got on the podium. Corser finished seventh behind Lavilla after retiring in the first race. Two curiosities: the 2003 championship had just got underway and already discussion was revolving around the 2004 rules, while the championship looked to have already been wrapped up by Ducati.

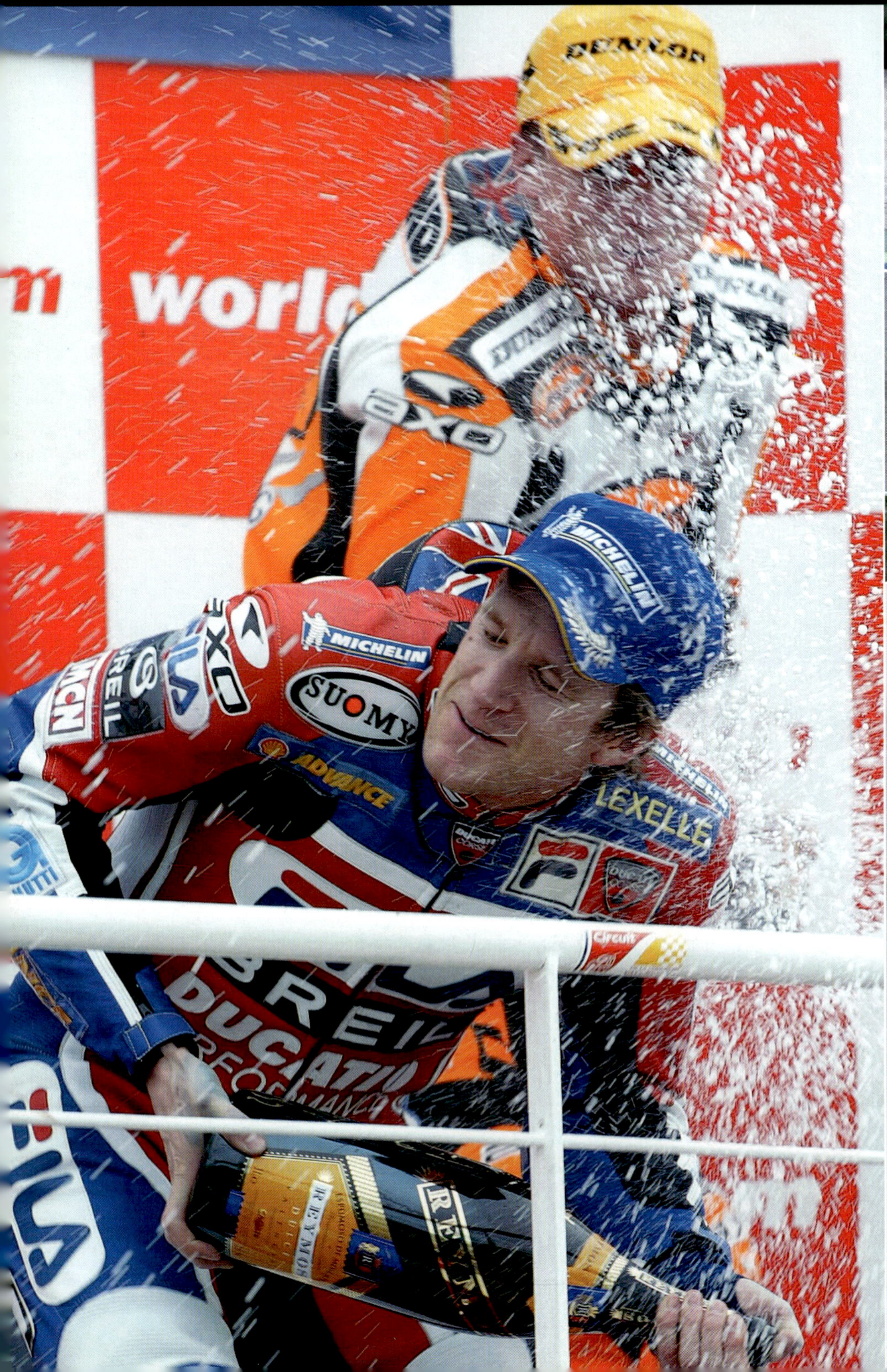

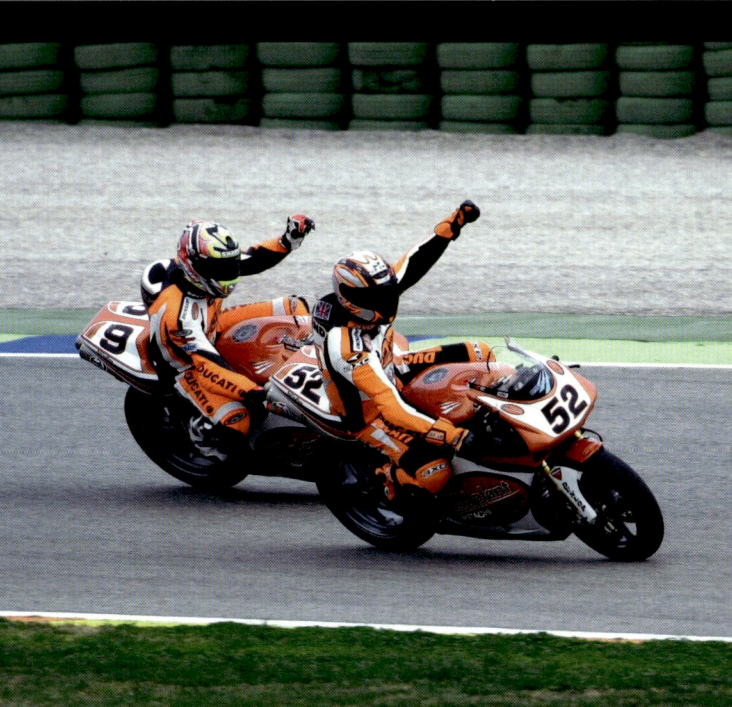

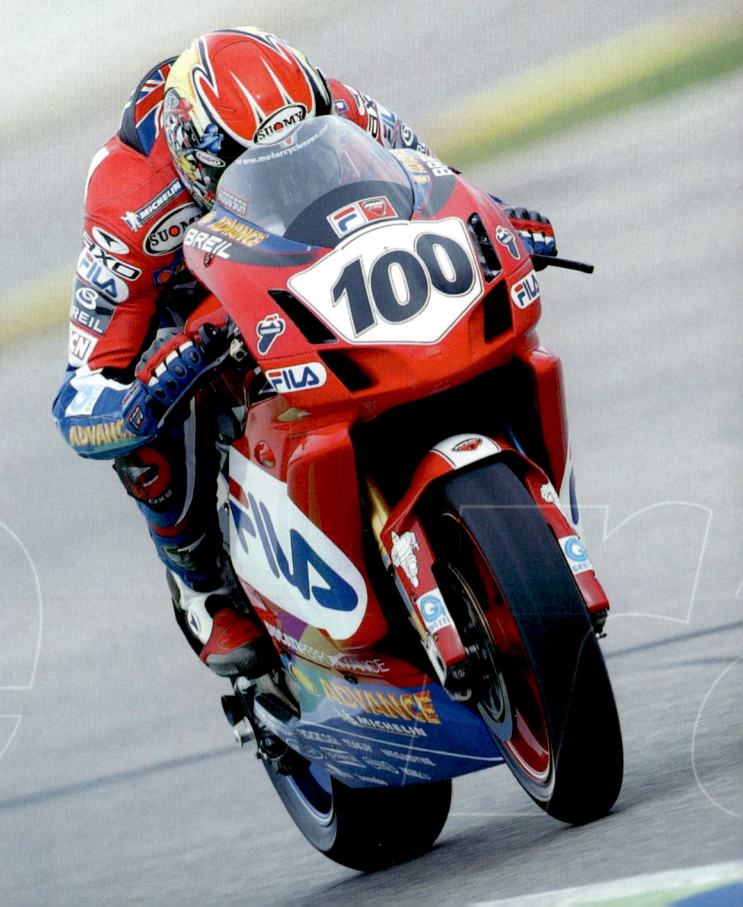

RACES Phillip Island (AUS) • 30/03/03

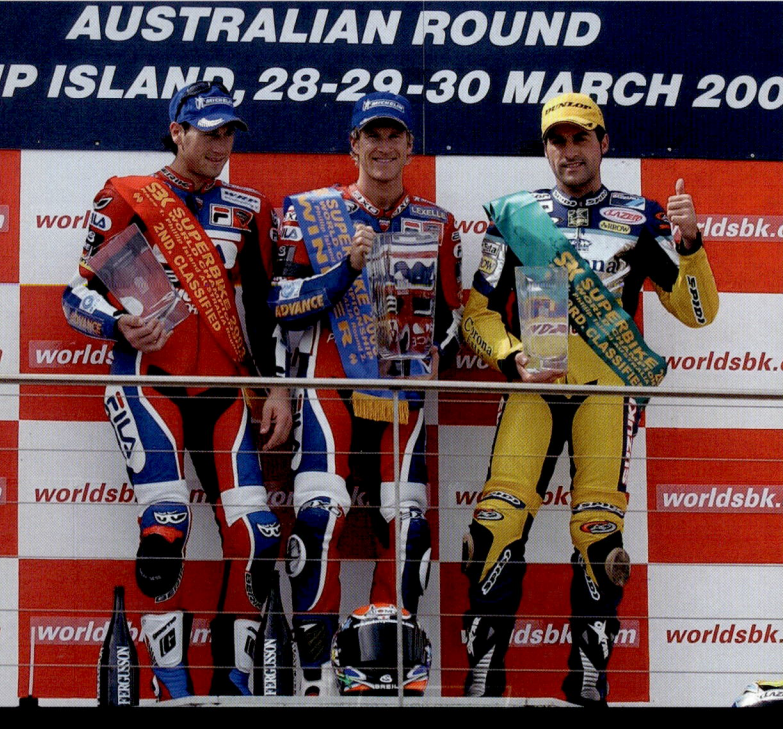

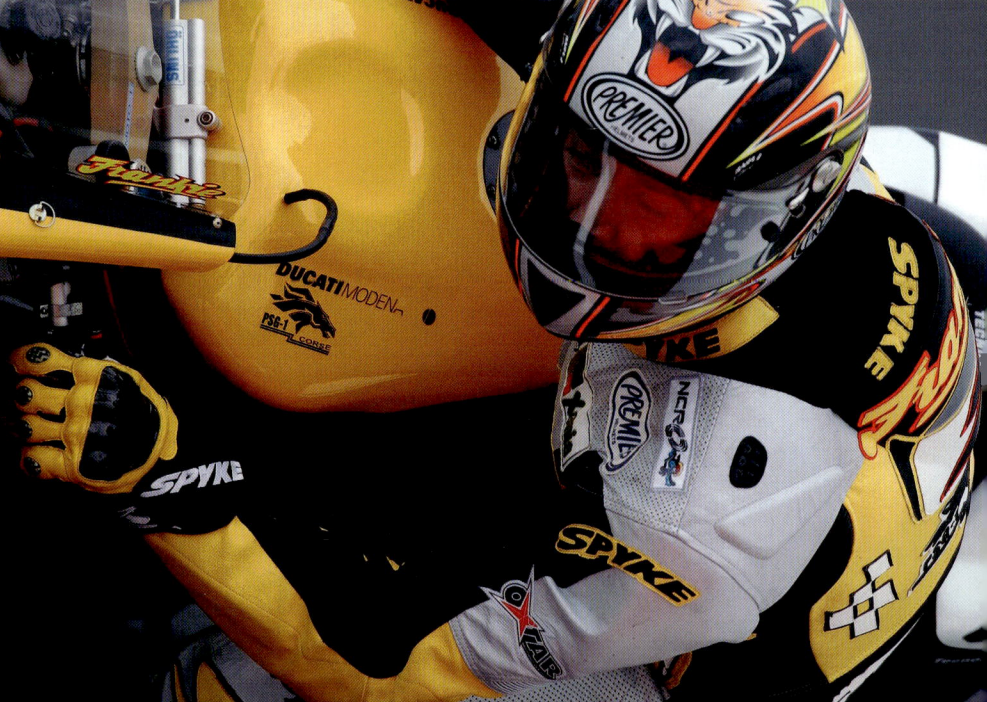

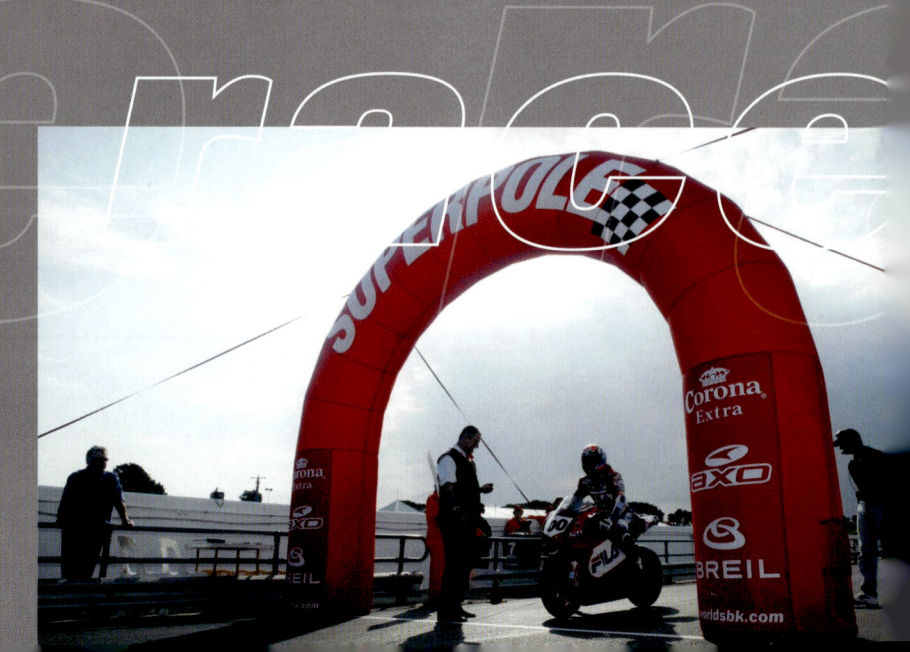

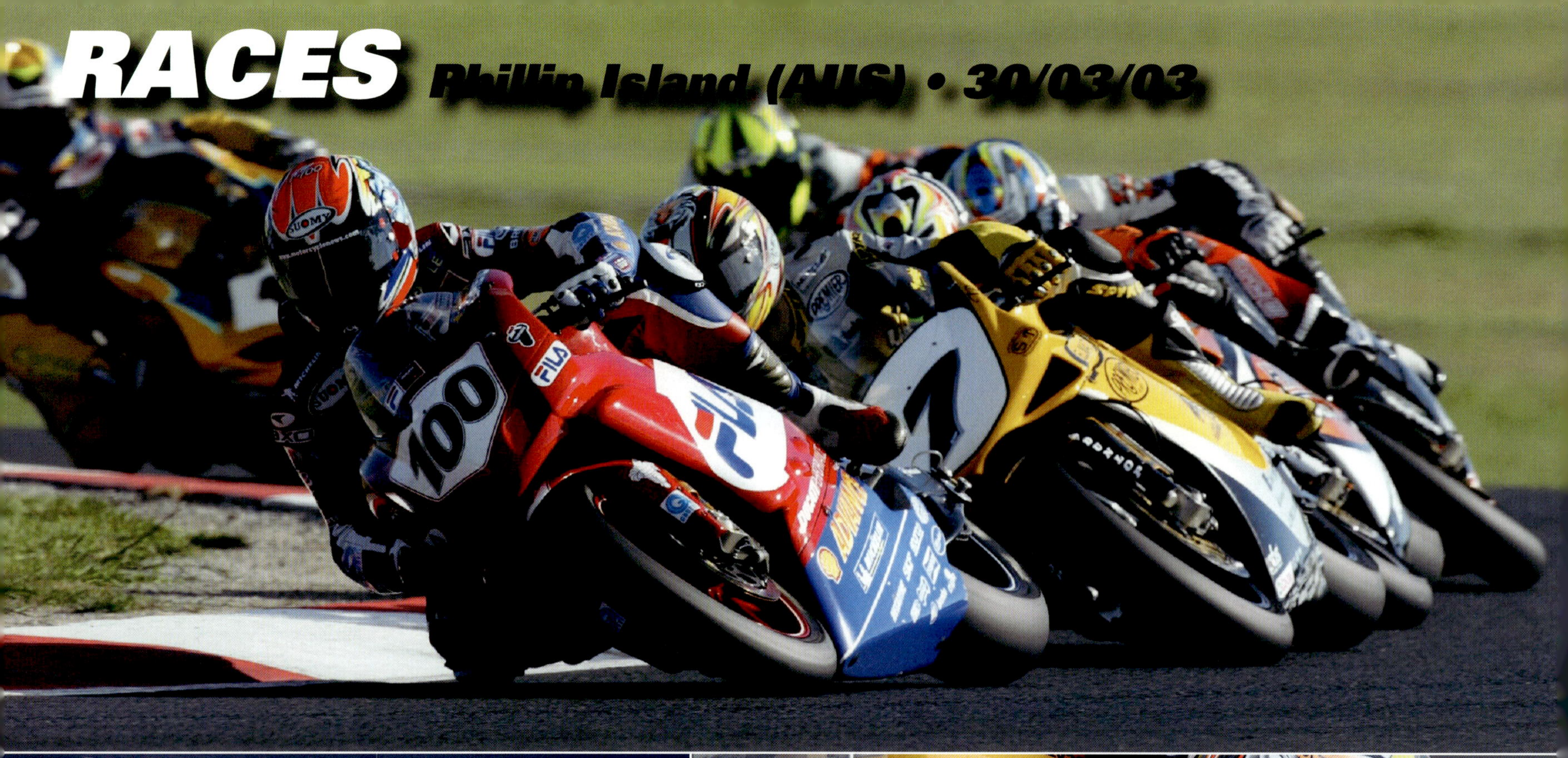

the race

Things remained the same at Phillip Island, at least regarding the name of the winner. Hodgson set pole position and won both races, with Xaus twice following him home as runner-up. WSBK 'veteran' Chili also performed well in Australia with a private Ducati, the Italian finishing on the podium after qualifying second behind Hodgson. Third place in race 1 went to Spain's Lavilla, on the podium for the first time since Misano 2001. This was a good result for the Alstare Suzuki GSX-R 1000 rider, but he could only finish seventh in race 2, while Corser twice scored points with the Petronas.

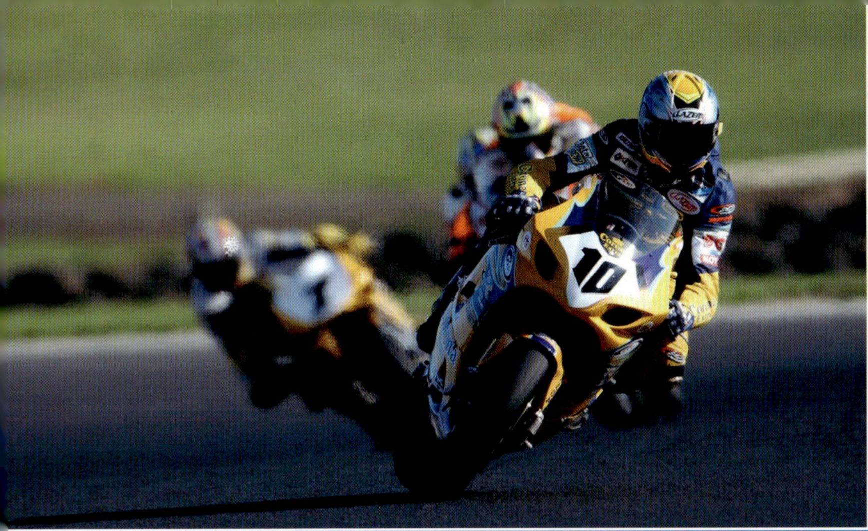

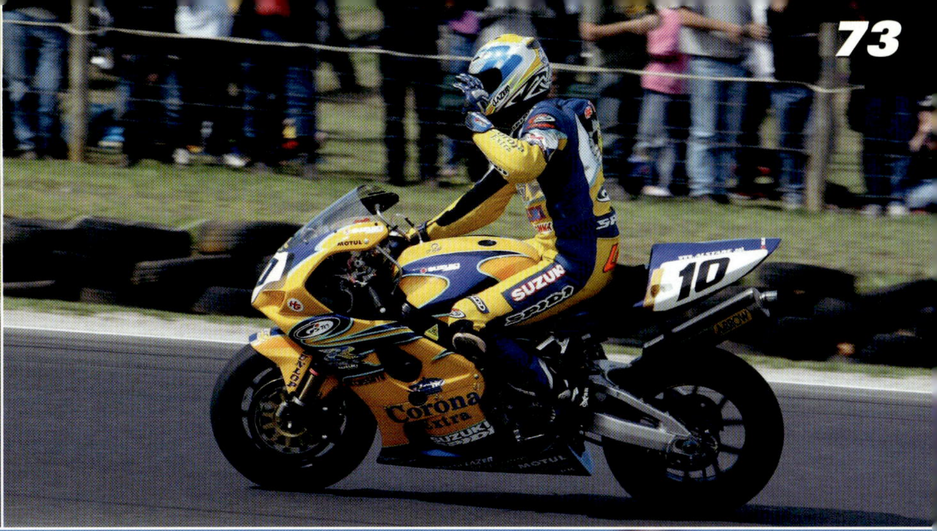
10
SUZUKI
Corona Extra

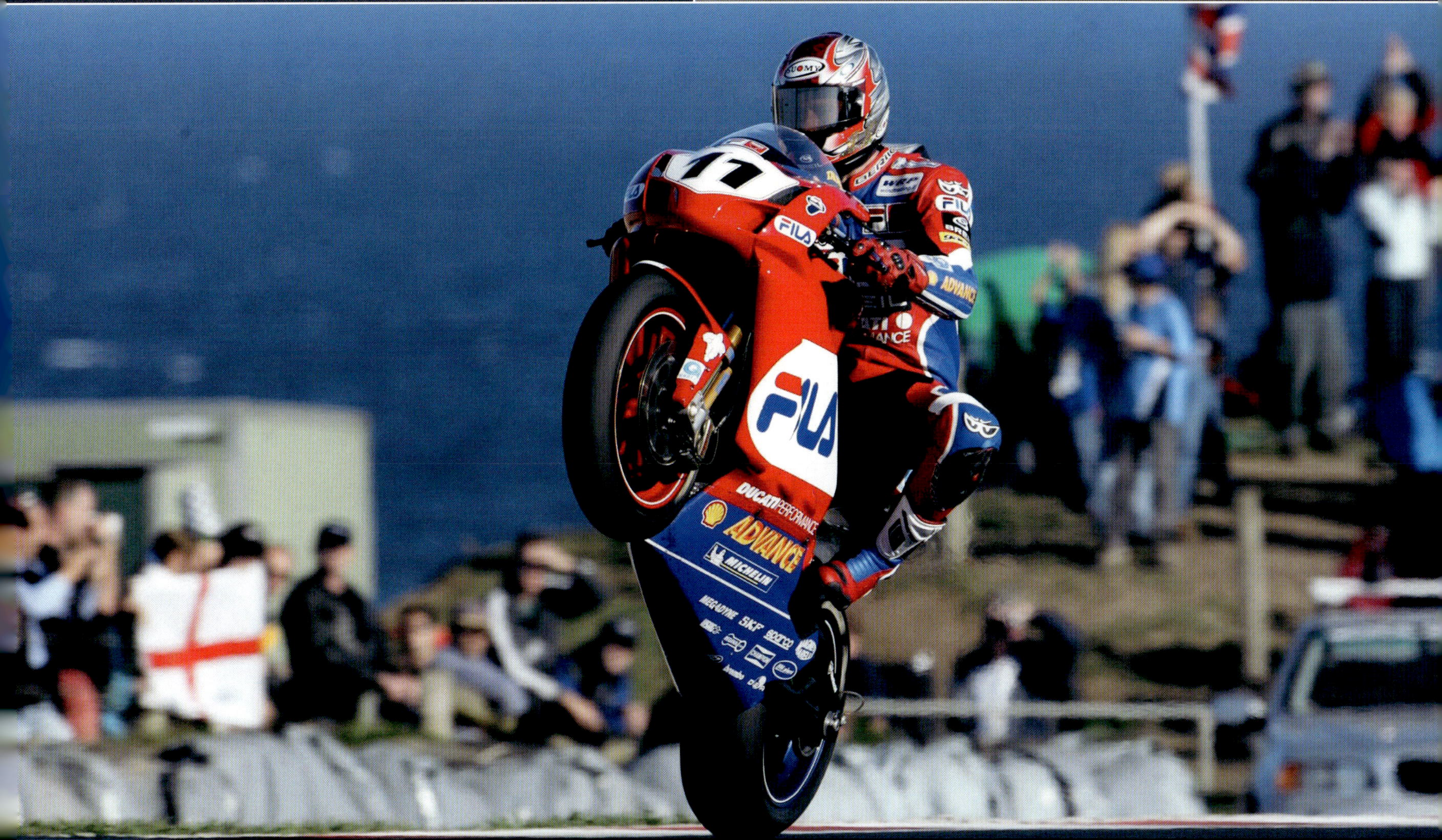
FILA
ADVANCE
MICHELIN

100

SUOMY
100

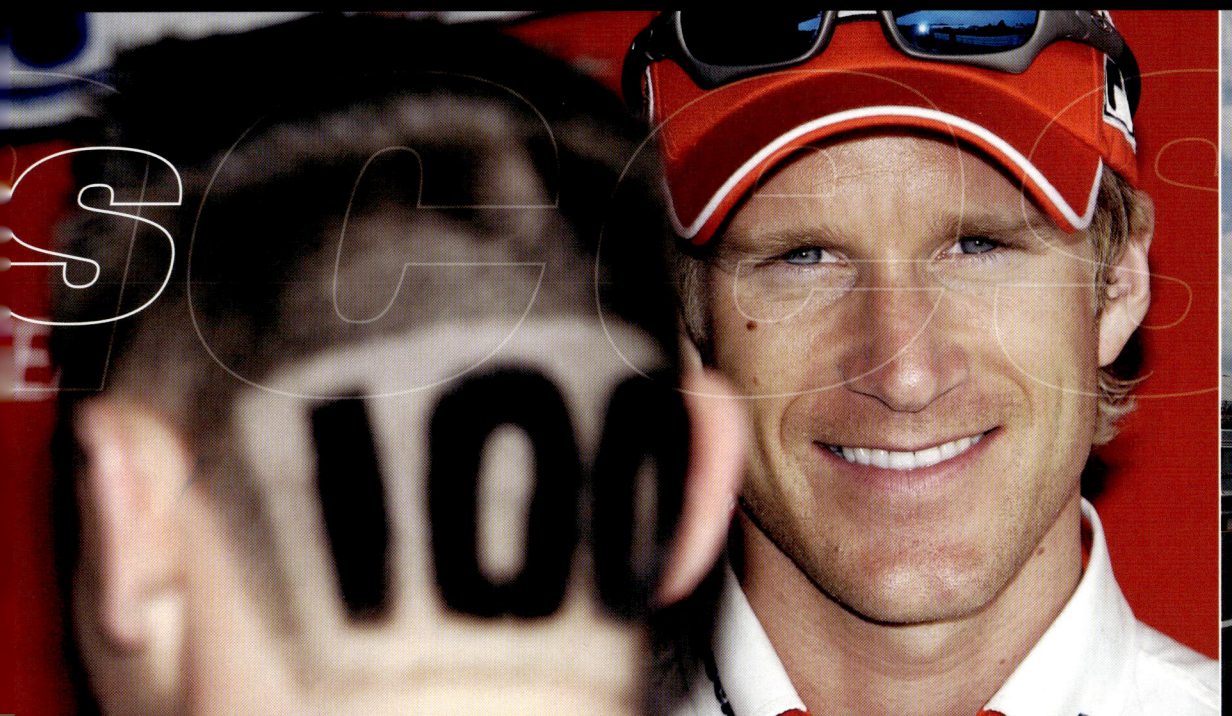

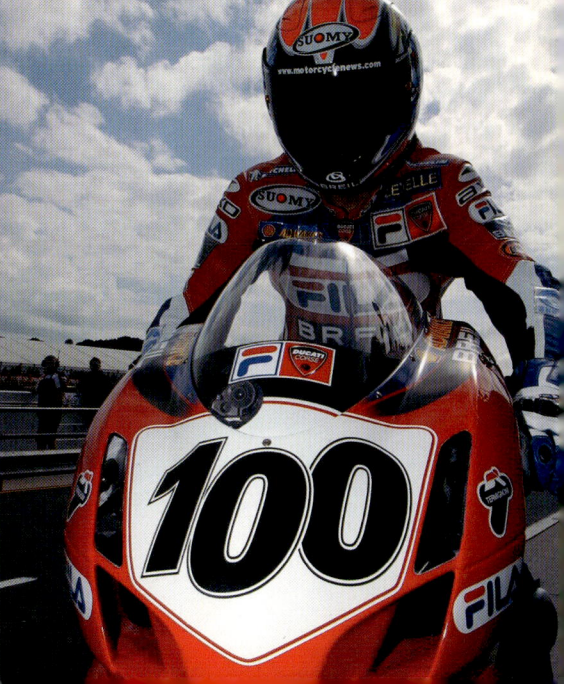

RACES Sugo (JPN) • 27/04/03

the race

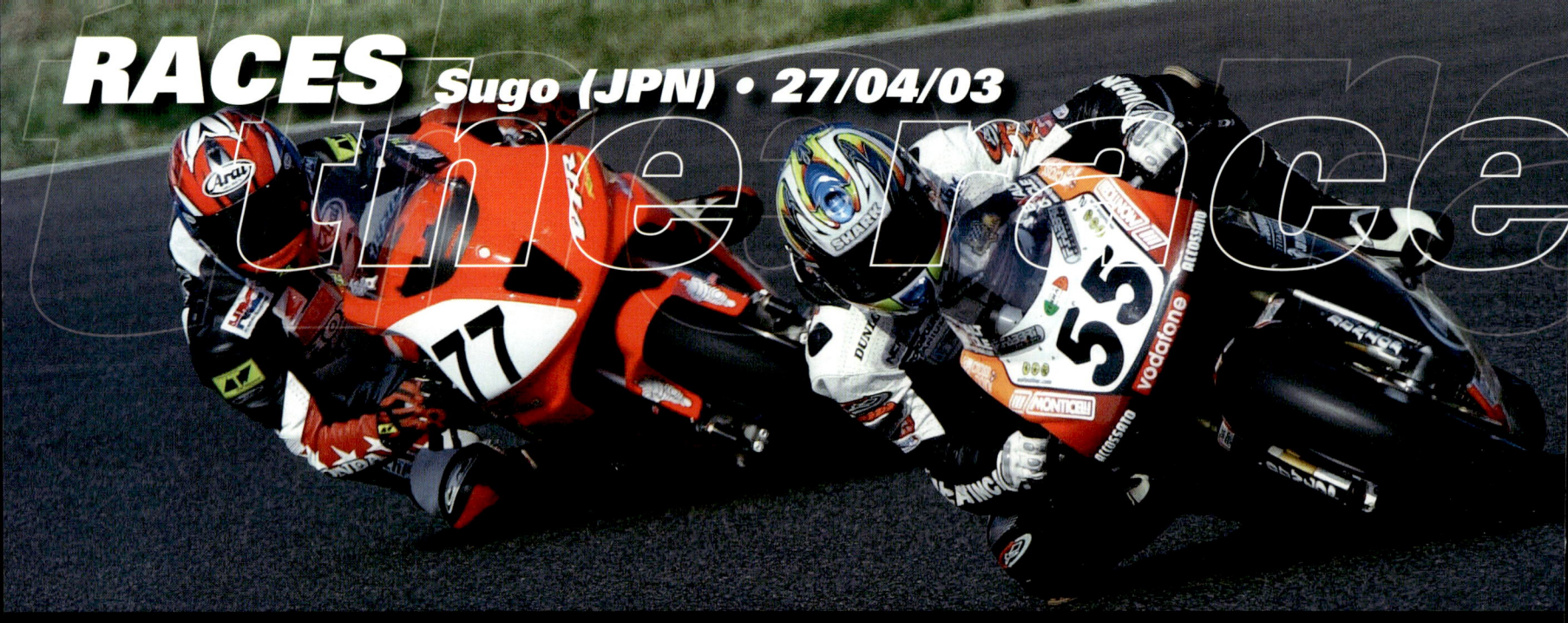

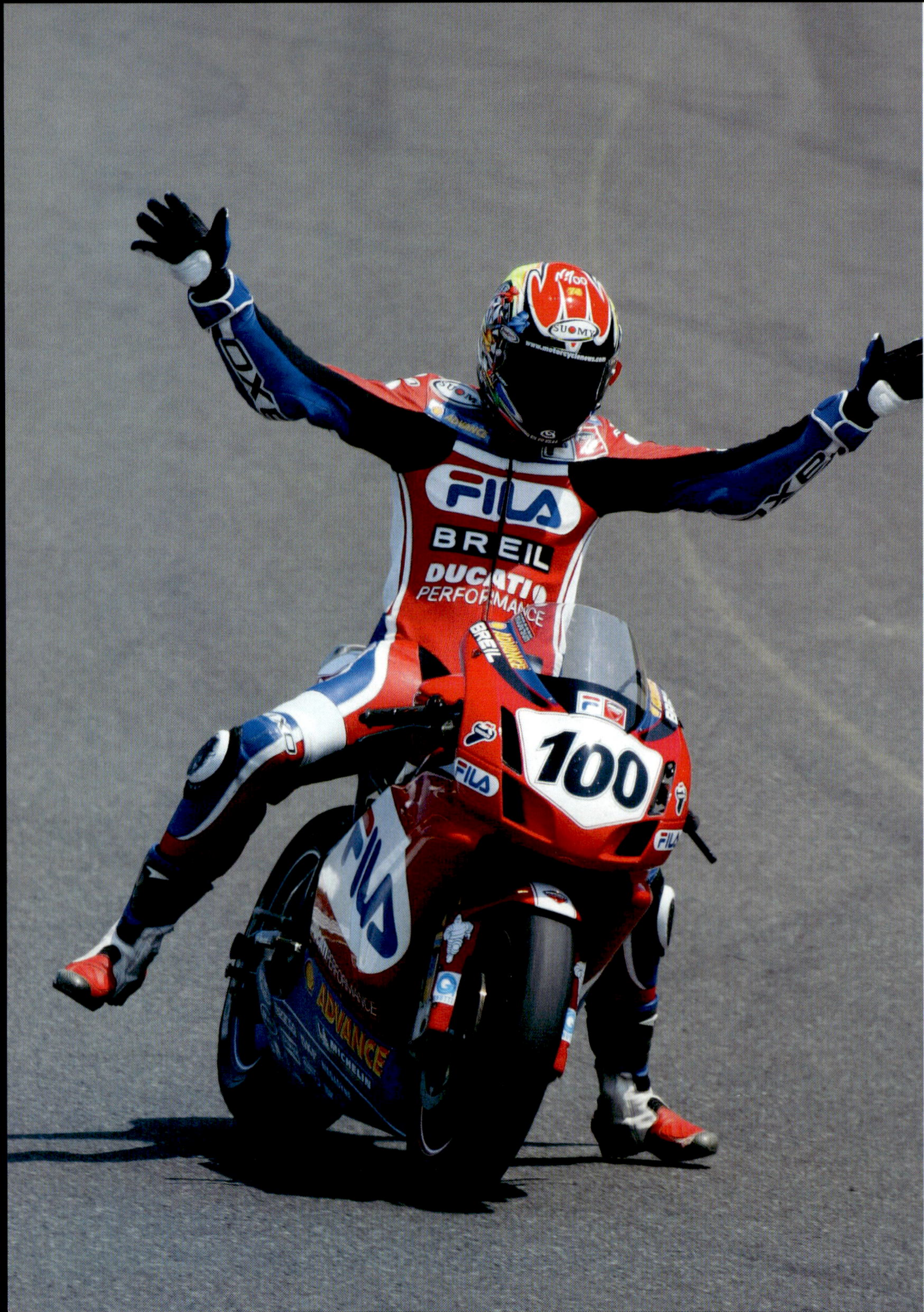

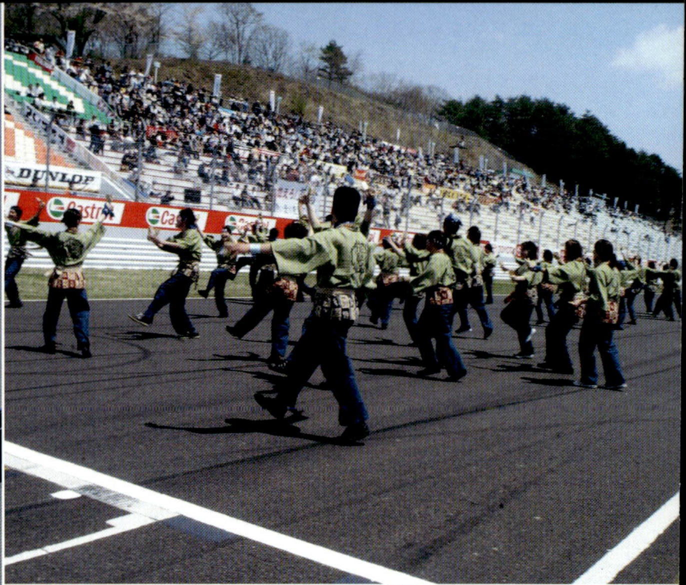

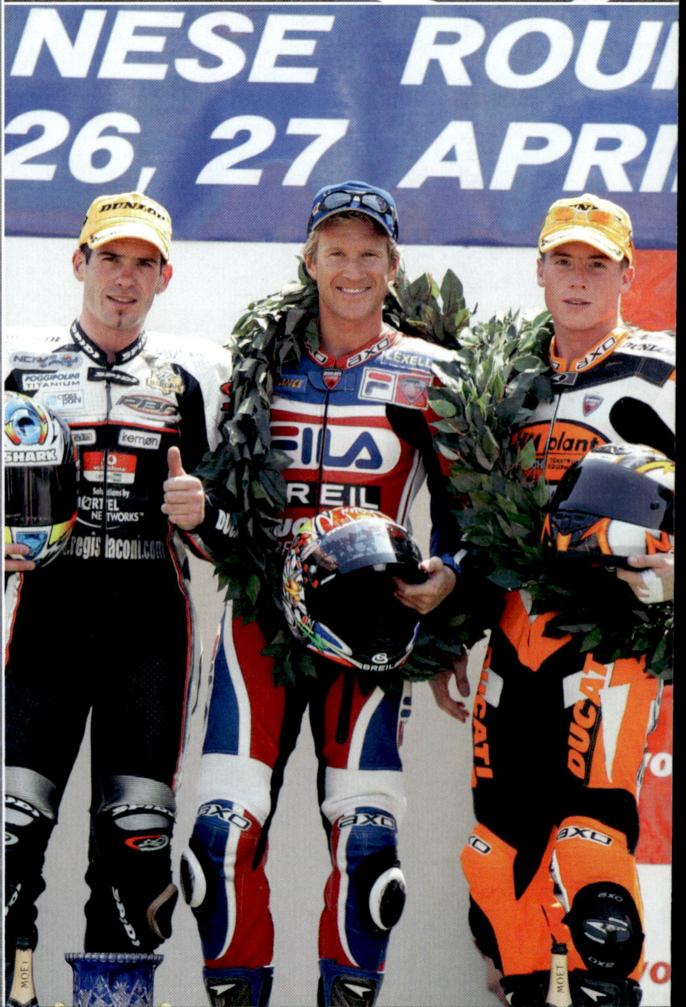

The ownership of the championship reverted completely to its previous promoters, the Flammini brothers, who took over from Octagon. On the track high expectation surrounded Izutsu's HRC Honda VTR1000, but the results were disappointing: ninth in qualifying and twice sixth in the races. Pole went to the surprising Frenchman Laconi ahead of Chili and Lavilla, but things were back to normal in the races with a double victory for Hodgson who easily controlled the situation. Lavilla

tried everything possible to win race 2 but failed by just 6/10ths of a second. Toseland picked up a third and a fifth while Chili was third in race 2. The Petronas continued to disappoint, with Corser retiring in race 1 and finishing twelfth in the second while Haydon picked up a ninth and a DNF in the two races.

the race

B ack to Europe and the legendary Monza circuit, but it was still Hodgson on the top of the world in qualifying and the races. Ducati dominated Superpole with four bikes on the front row; Hodgson, Chili, Toseland and Laconi. Suzuki had high hopes of a good race with Lavilla fifth and the young Italian talent Iannuzzo eighth, while Xaus had a spectacular crash, luckily without any serious consequences. With his two Monza wins, Neil notched up a maximum 200 points, almost double that of his teammate Xaus, while Ducati celebrated its 200th win in World

Superbike. Just four-tenths of a second split the top four finishers in race 1: Hodgson, Laconi, Lavilla and Toseland. Lavilla then pulled out all the stops to finish 44/1000ths of a second behind the British champion in race 2, while Iannuzzo had a good race to finish ninth.

RACES Oschersleben (GER) • 01/06/03

The first upset of the season came when Toseland, who had gone close to winning in Oschersleben race 1, clinched victory after the break. Hodgson set pole ahead of Chili and Toseland in qualifying and that was the way they finished in race 1. Chili had electrical problems in the second race and was unable to go any higher than eleventh, while Toseland took his maiden WSBK win ahead of Hodgson and Walker. Xaus had an off-day with a DNF and a fifth place in the two German races, while the Petronas were again off the pace. Attention off the track revolved around the 2004 regulations, which were thought to include an abolition of the air restrictors.

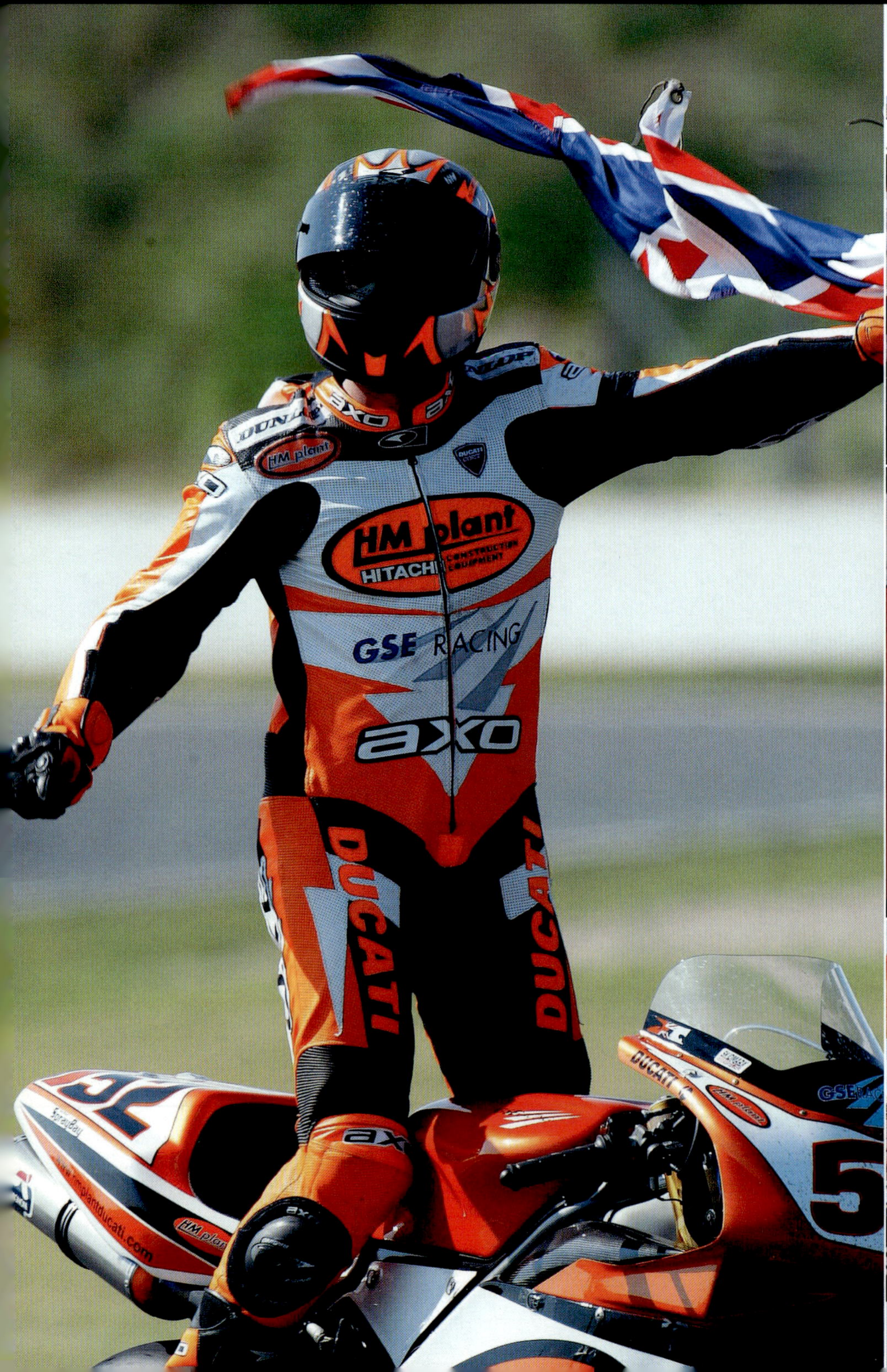

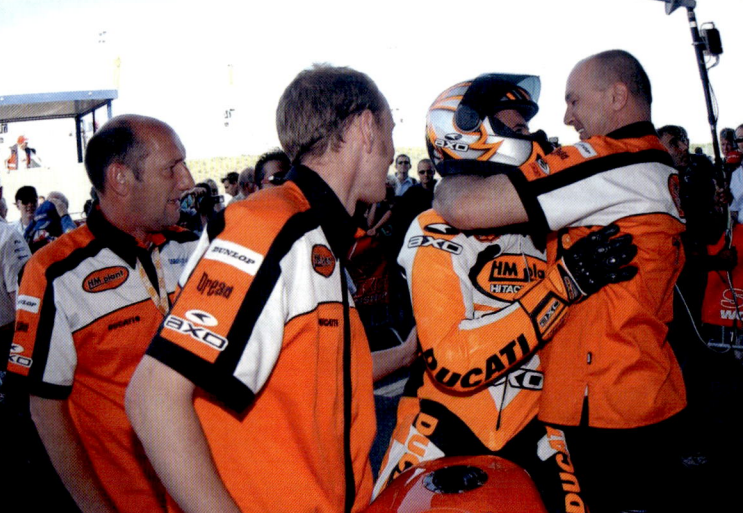

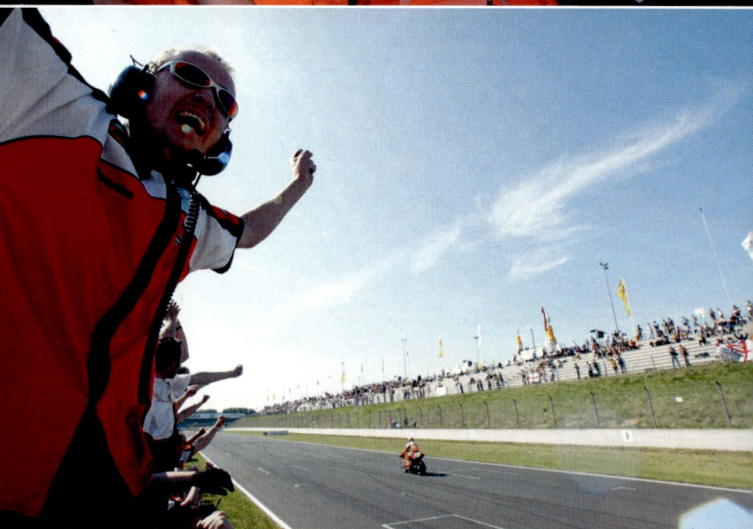

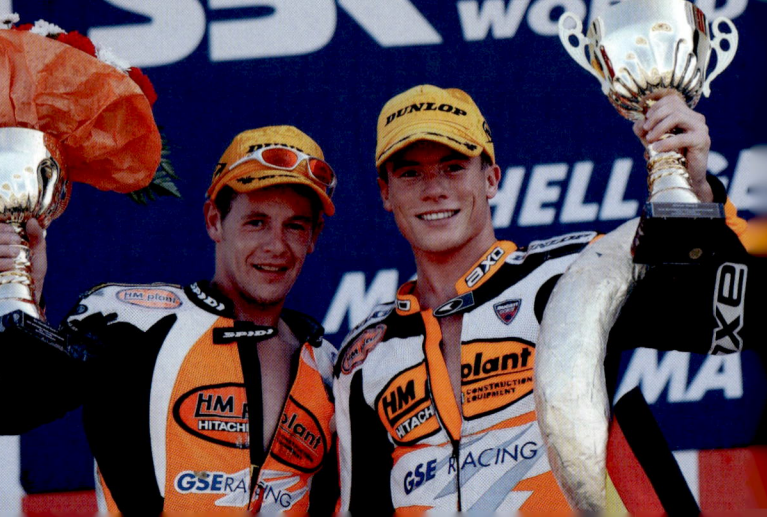

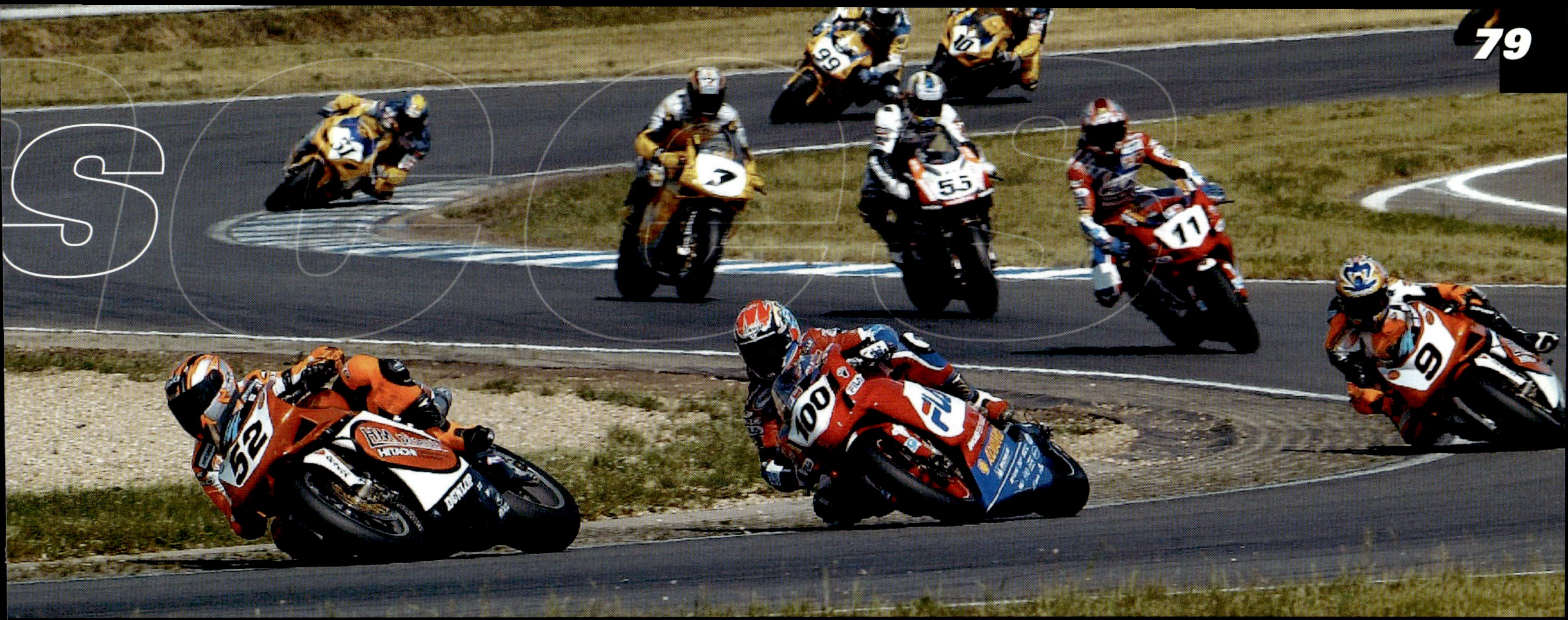

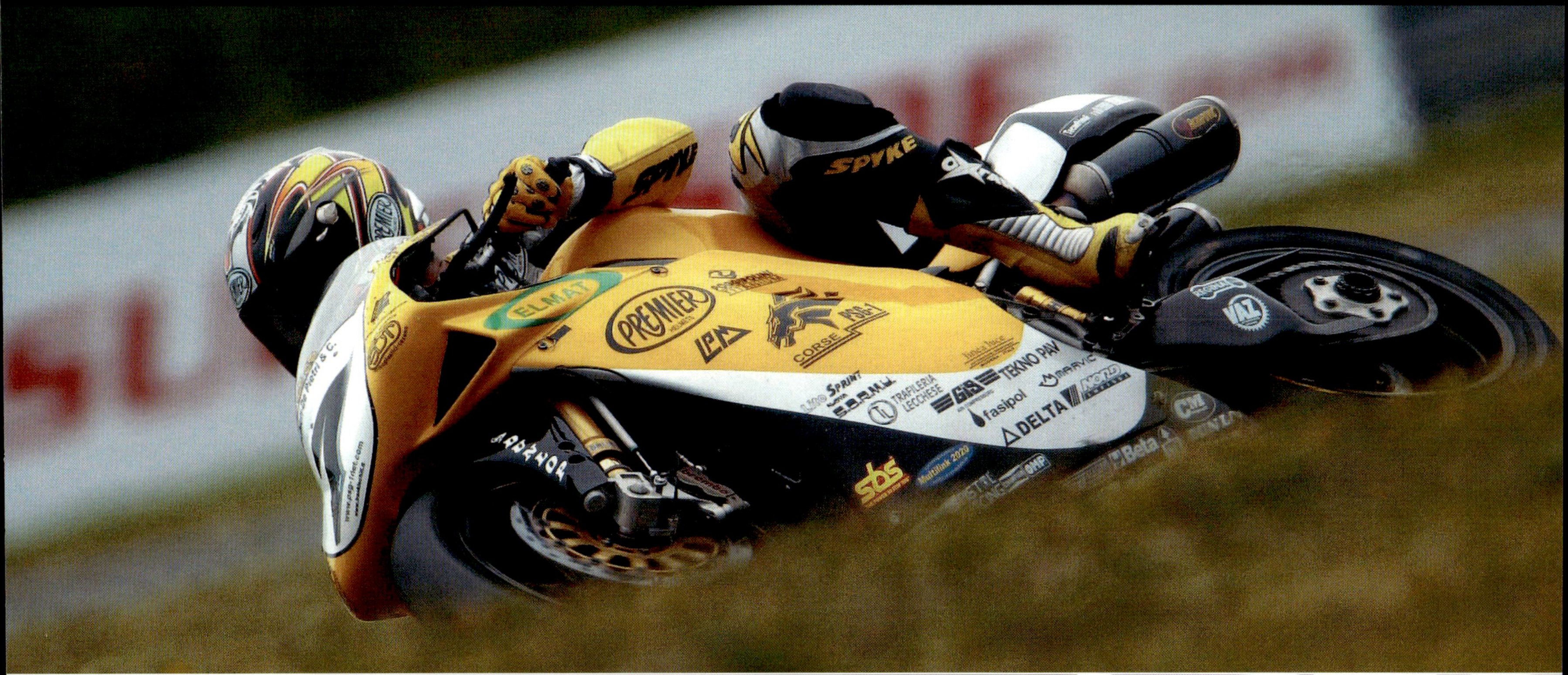
SPYKE
ELMAT
PREMIER
TRAFILERIA LECCHESE
fasipol
DELTA
sbs

100
FILA

SB
FILA
BREIL

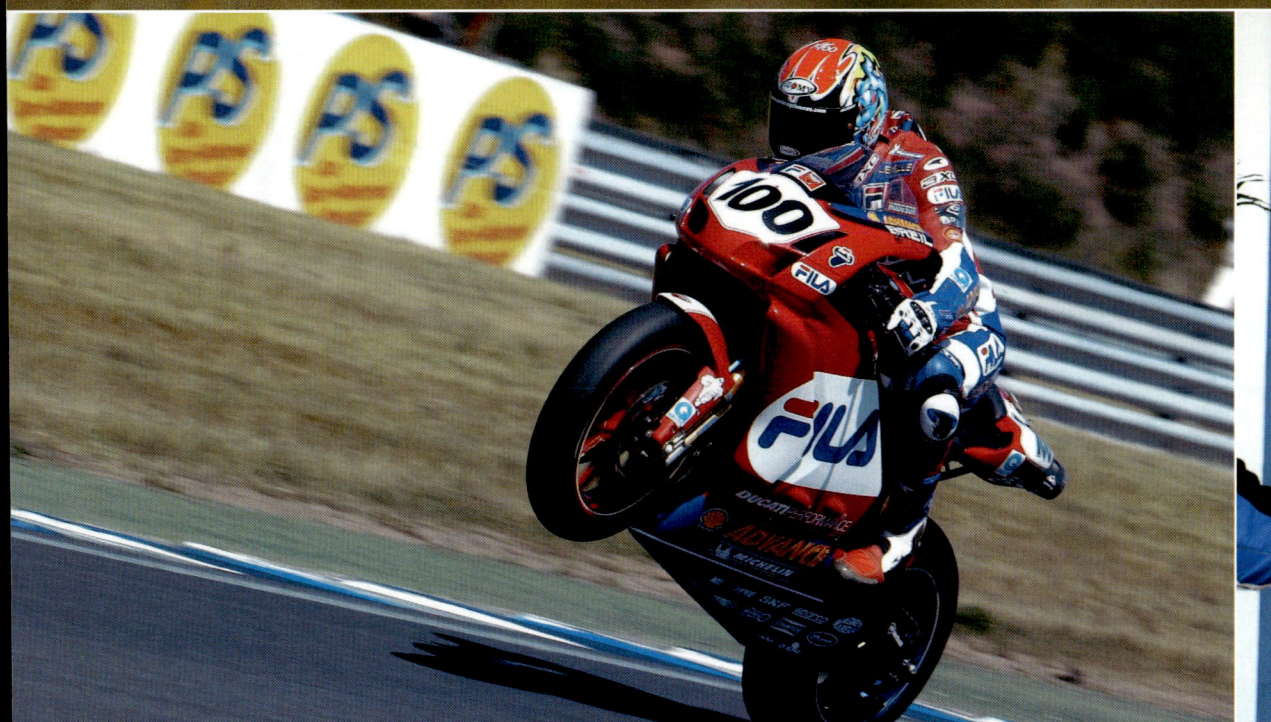

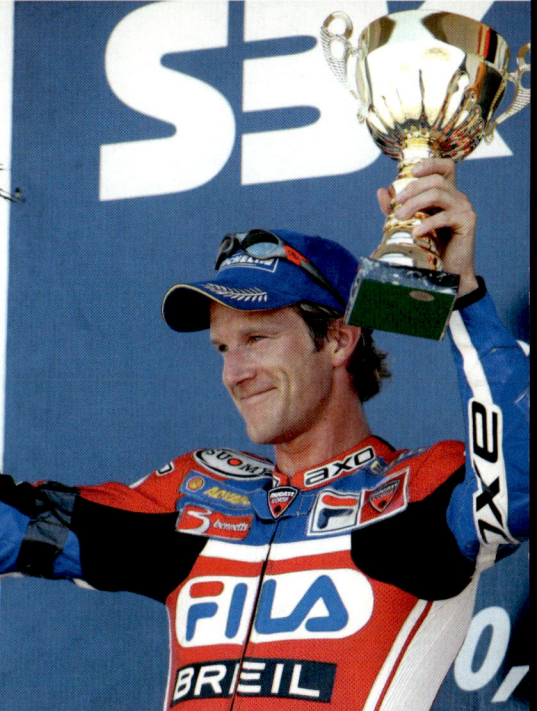

the race

55
11
52
100
FILA

100
SUOMY
BREIL
FILA
Corona

FILA
BREIL
MCN
Red Bull
Renegade

SBK
SUPERBIKE WORLD CHAMPIONSHIP
FGSPORT

The 80,000 spectators present at Silverstone were anxiously waiting for the performance of Suzuki-Rizla's Yukio Kagayama, the Japanese rider who had set the British championship alight, and he didn't disappoint, with second quickest time in qualifying behind Hodgson and ahead of Laconi, Lavilla, Rutter et al. Toseland succeeded in finishing behind Hodgson in race 1, but ahead of Xaus. The Suzuki challenge faded away and while Lavilla crashed, Kagayama finished fifth. The Japanese rider obtained the same result in race 1, while this time Lavilla finished right behind Hodgson but ahead of Xaus and Toseland.

Anyone who thought that Xaus was in the midst of a crisis period had to think again at the Misano round, where the Spanish rider won both races. Pole had gone to Hodgson, who edged out Chili in front of his home crowd, Toseland and an amazing Iannuzzo, while Corser (Petronas) was eighth. On lap 2 the current championship leader sensationally crashed out of the race, leaving Chili the task of battling with Xaus, but the Italian also crashed out on the last lap and the win went to the Ducati Fila rider. Hodgson had to take second best to Xaus in race 2, finishing ahead of Chili, Laconi and Lavilla, while Iannuzzo was seventh with the Suzuki-Alstare.

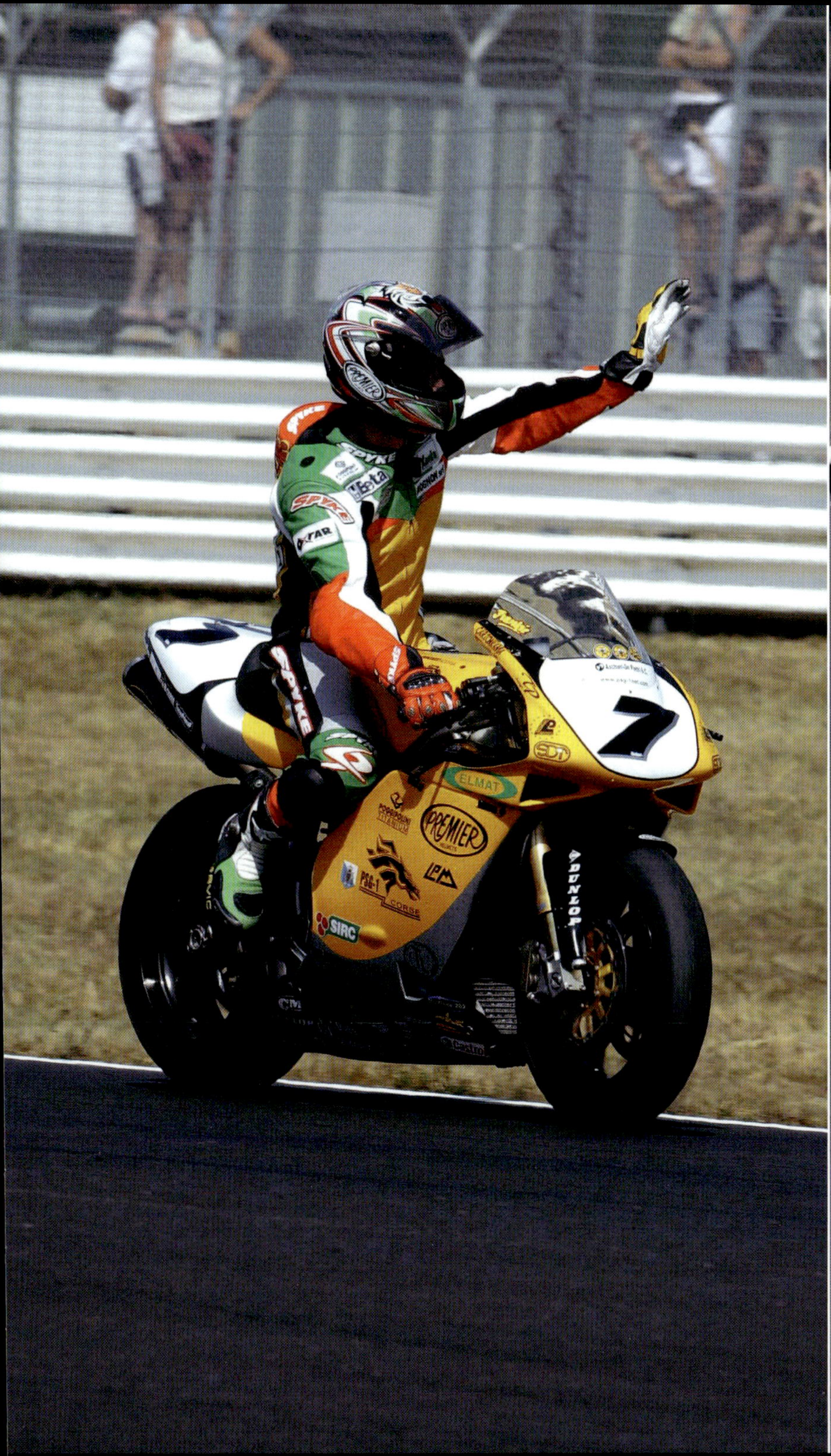
7
PREMIER
ELMAT
DUNLOP
SIRC

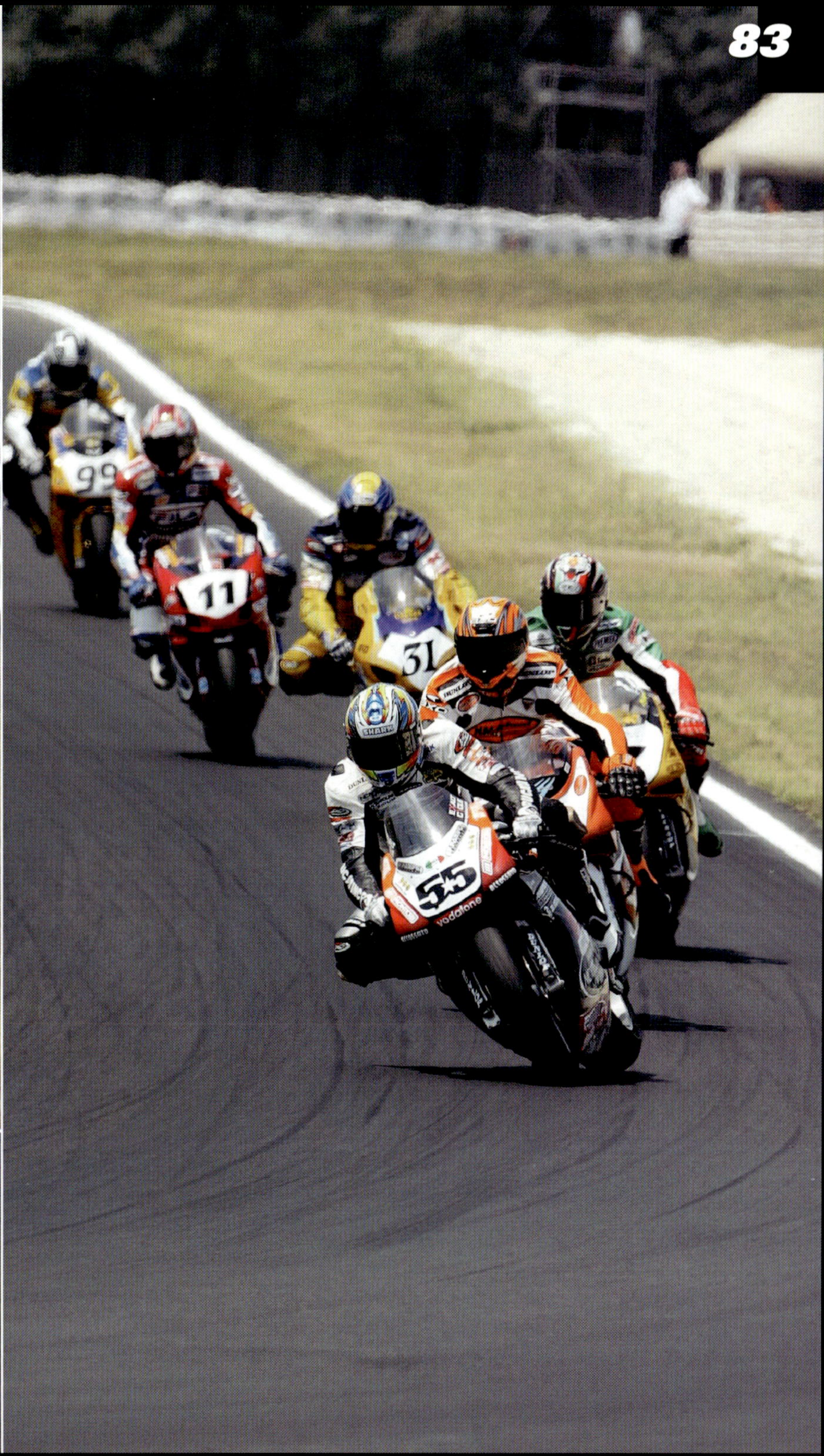
99
11
31
55
vodafone

7
555
31
100

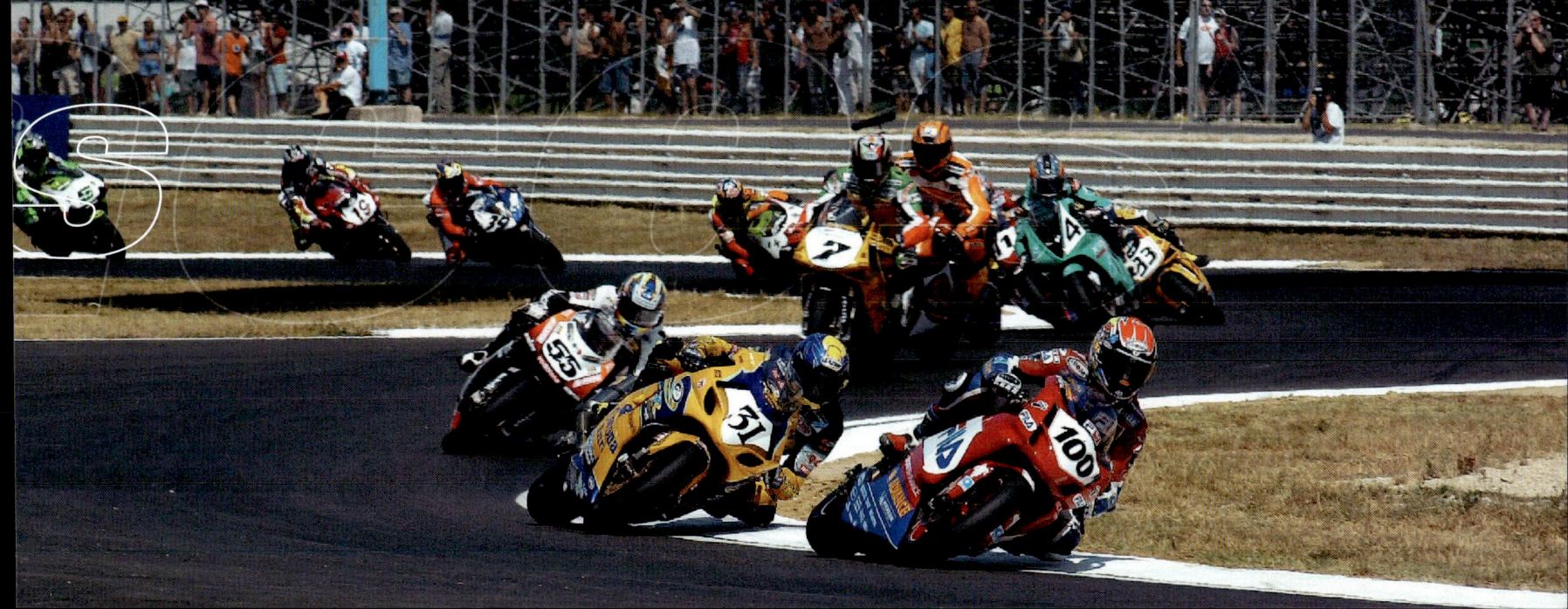

RACES Laguna Seca (USA) • 13/07/03

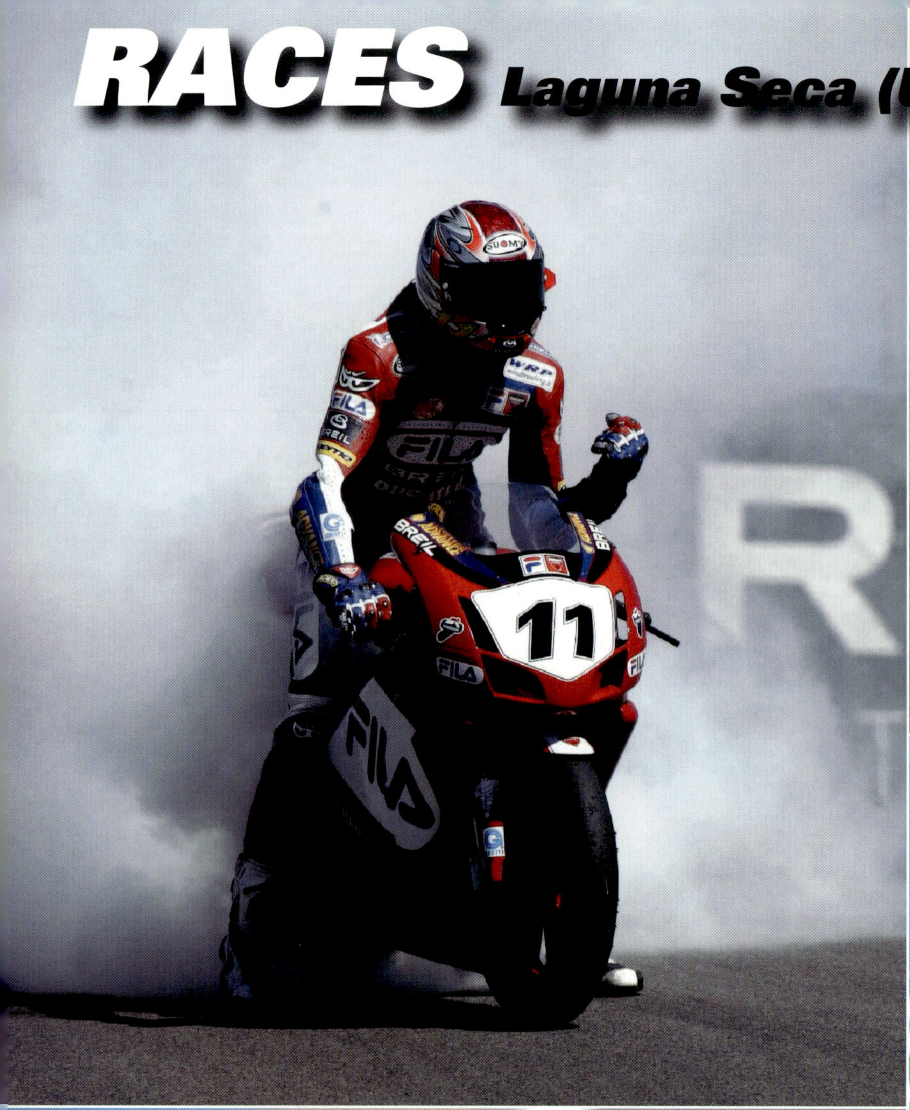

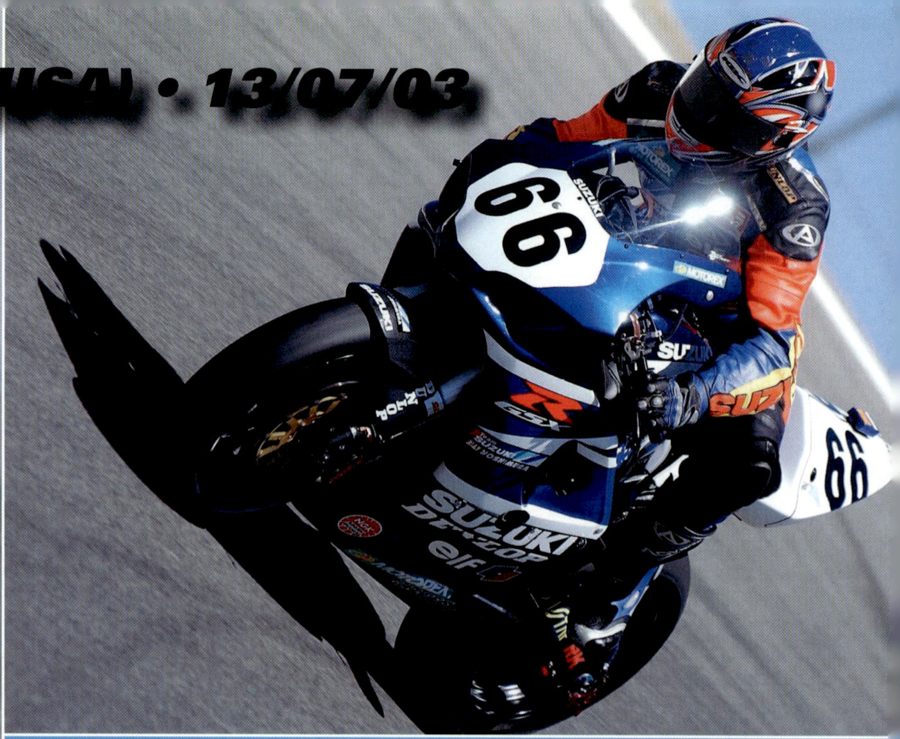

the race

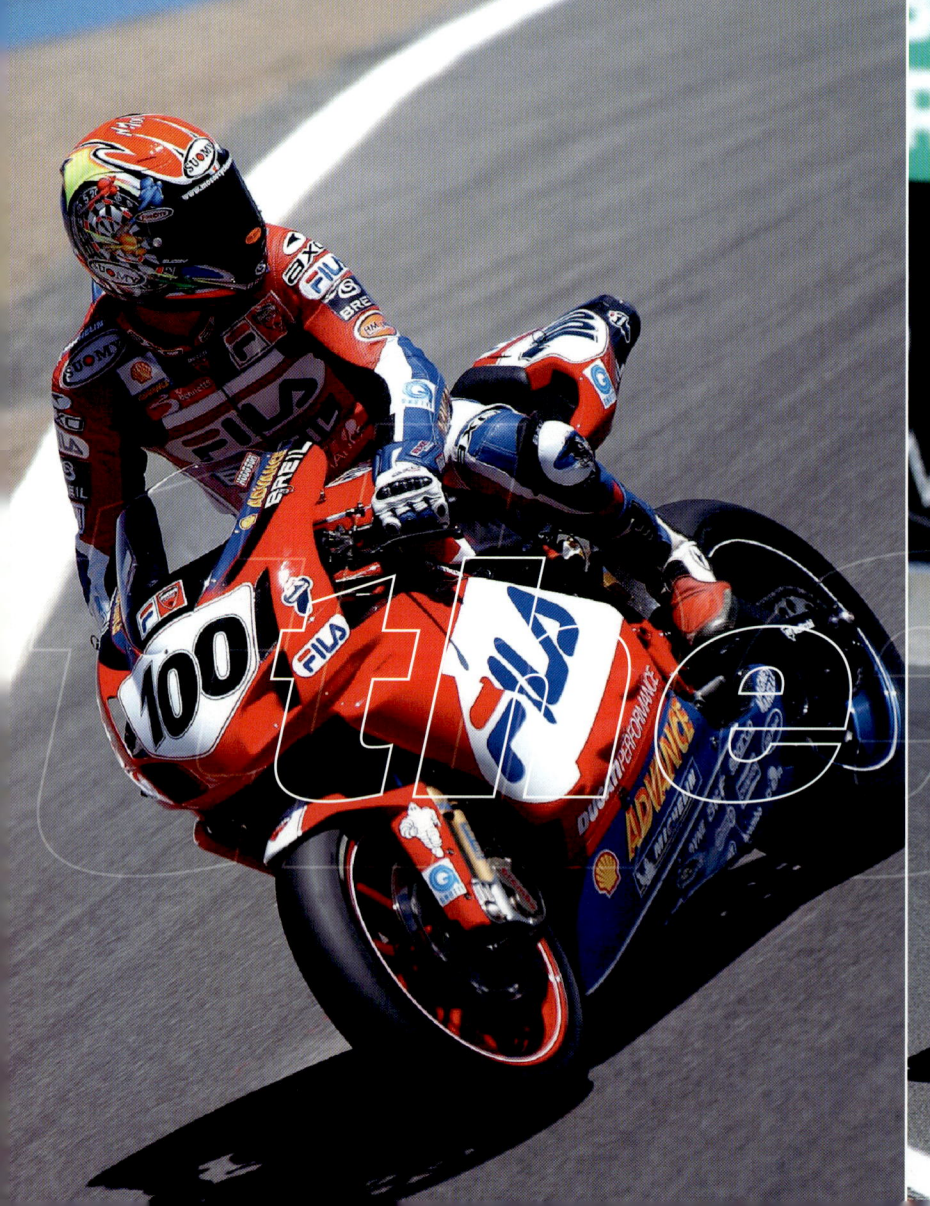

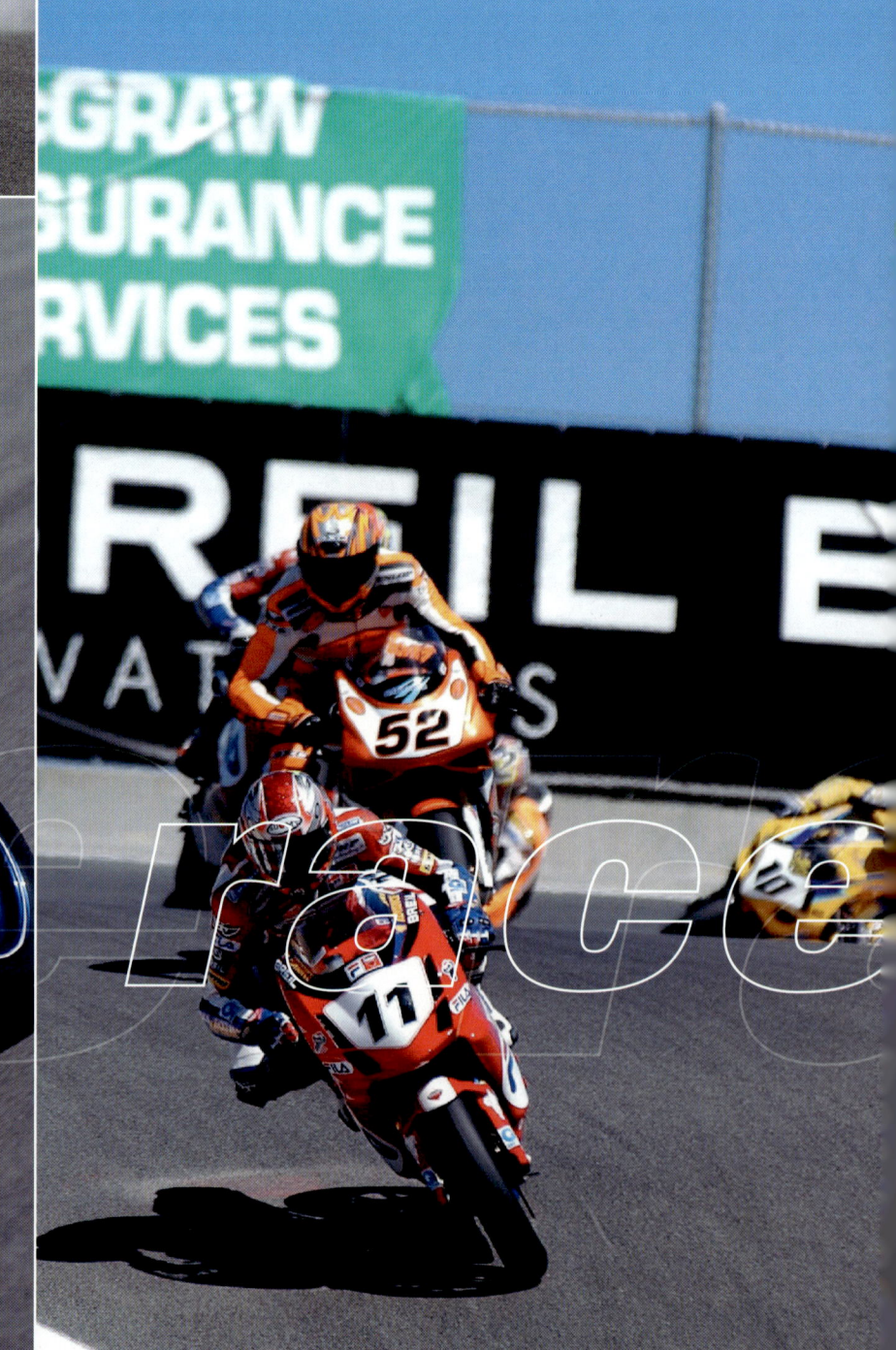

Very little of what happened on the Laguna Seca track will remain in the minds of the Superbike circus as the news of the new 2004 rules and the introduction of a one-make tyre rule was announced. For the record however the actual racing did provide good entertainment. Pole position was set by 32 year-old Mladin (Suzuki), ahead of team-mate Yates, Laconi and Bussei on his debut with the Ducati Austin bike; Xaus could only manage seventh while Hodgson was ninth. Chili took a fantastic win in race 1 from Hodgson and Toseland, while Mladin, with one eye on the AMA title race, finished fourth and Corser eighth. Xaus crashed out while in the lead, but then went on to win the second race from Hodgson and Walker. Lavilla took the four-cylinder Suzuki to fifth place, while Mladin did not line up for the start and Chili emerged unscathed from a nasty highside.

RACES Brands Hatch • (EUR) 27/07/03

Expectation was high over the second British round of the championship, where local riders always provide stiff opposition; and it was 'wild-card' John Reynolds who set pole with the Rizla Suzuki GSX-R ahead of Chris Walker and another 'wild-card', Shane Byrne. Hodgson meanwhile was only eleventh quickest. MonsterMob Ducati's Byrne then went on to score a superb double win, clinching the 2003 Manufacturers' title for Ducati after the British rider held off the challenge from a number of tough rivals.

Hodgson was unable to do any better than the runner-up slot in race 1, six seconds behind Byrne, followed by fifth in race 2. With Ducatis filling most of the top places, Reynolds got a good result for Suzuki, finishing second in a sprint to the line behind Byrne.

BRANDS HATCH
25, 26, ?? JULY 2003

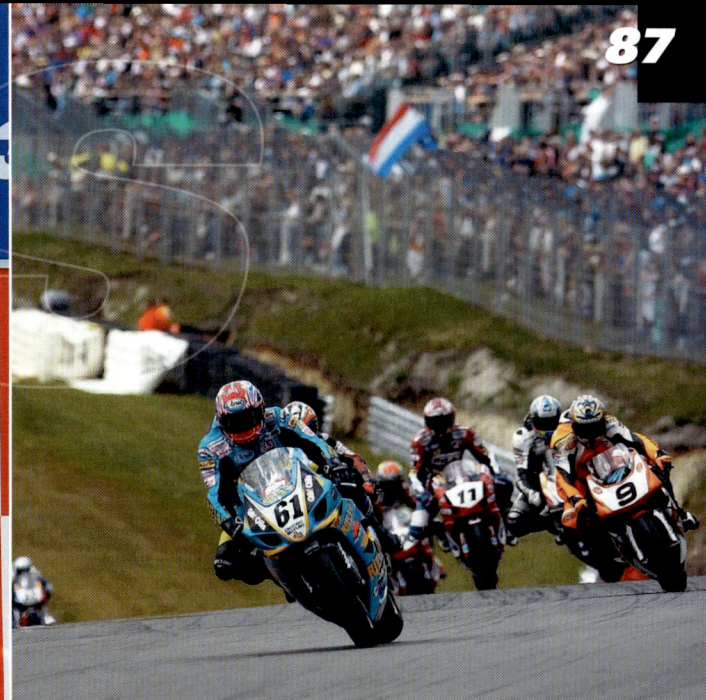

the race

11
FILA

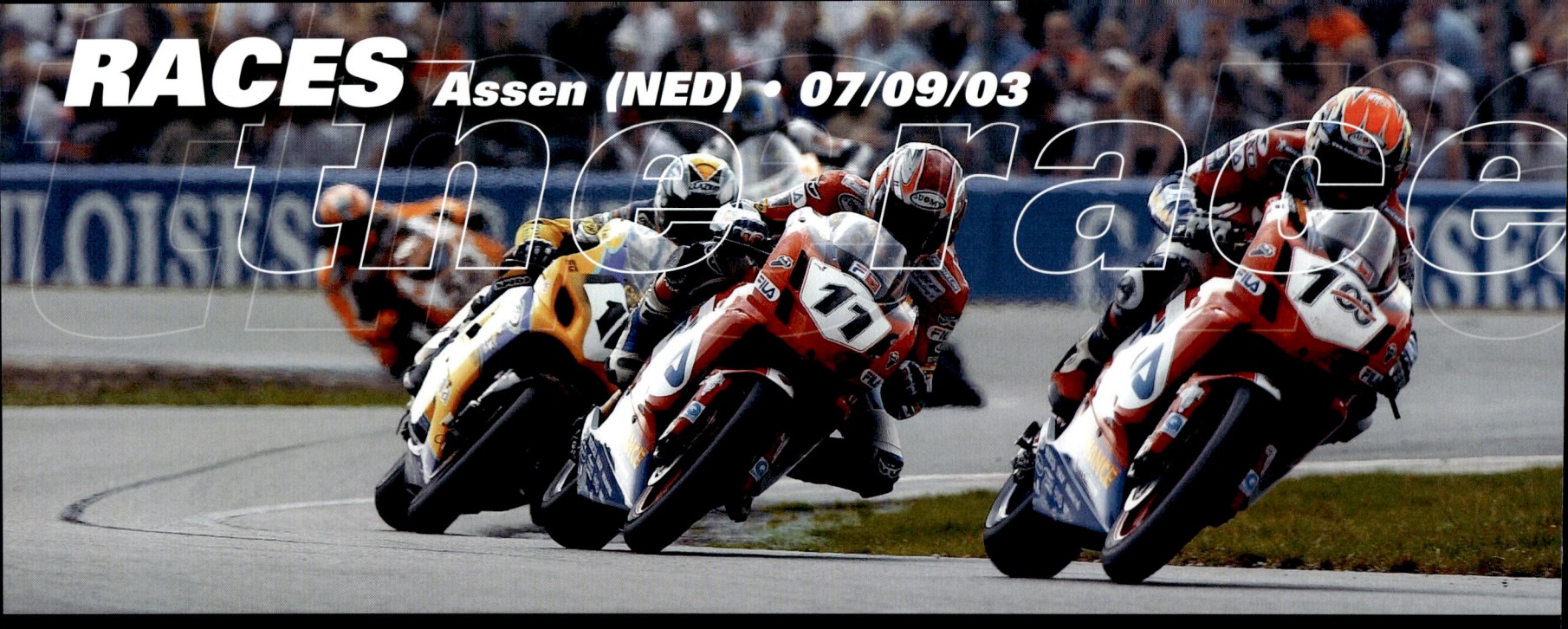

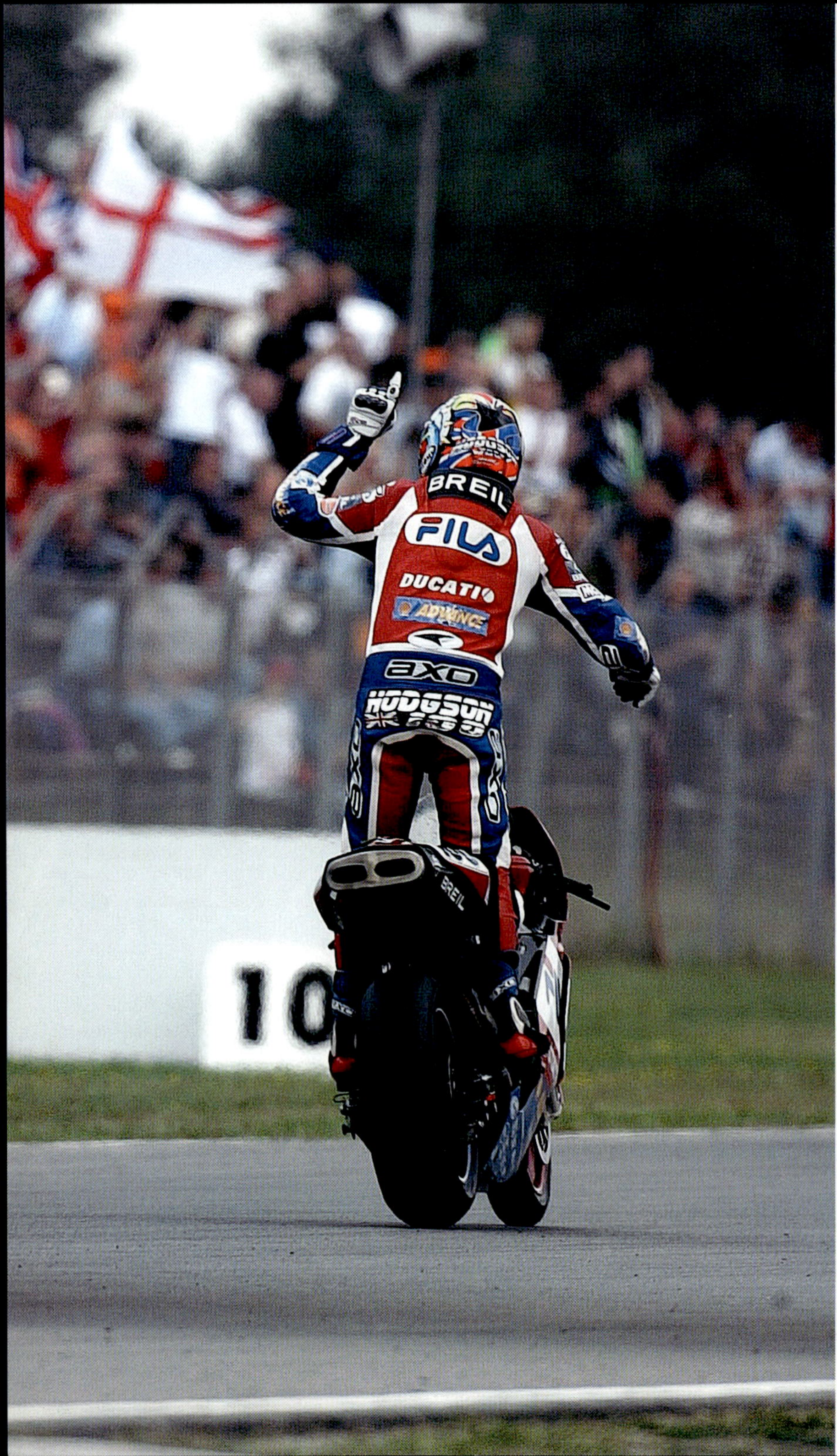
BREIL
FILA
DUCATI
ADVANCE
AXO
HODGSON
10

DUCATI
CORSE
FILA

11
FILA
STAYER
ADVANCE
MICHELIN

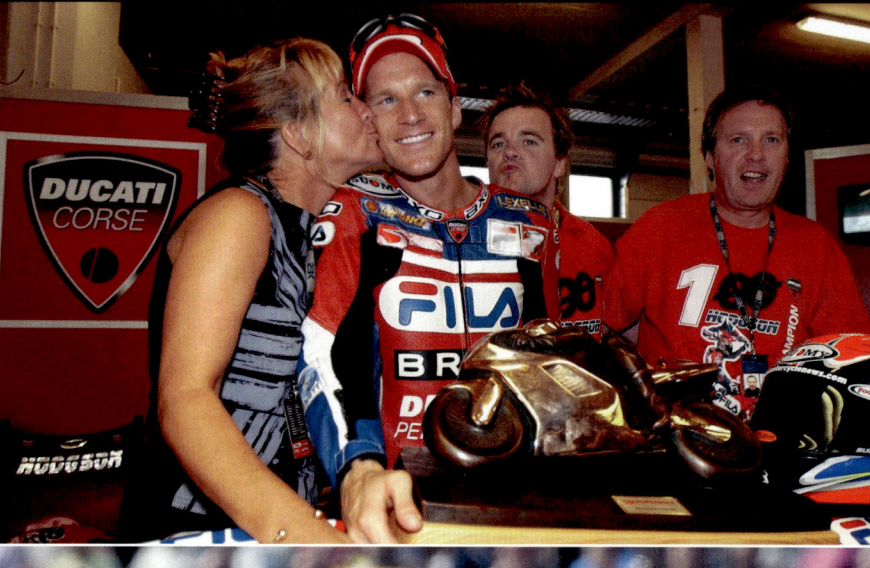

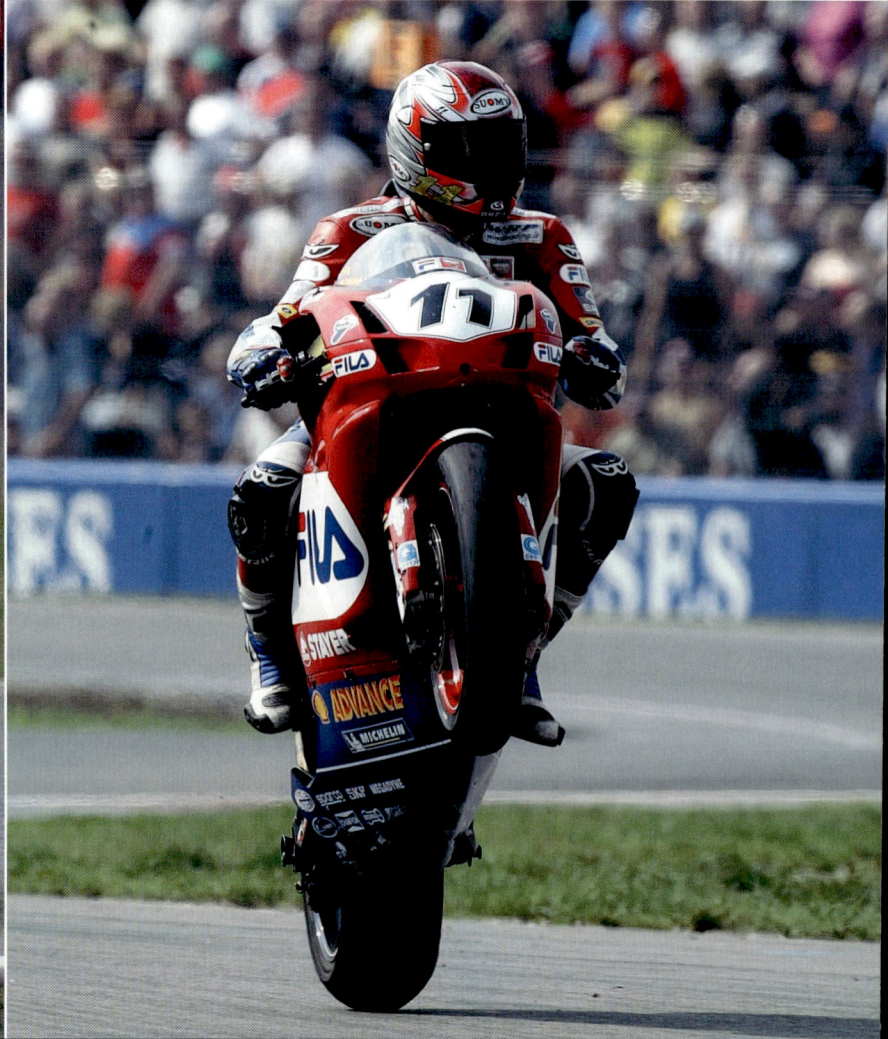

After a month's break the world championship came to Assen, where Hodgson could clinch the 2003 title. Pole went to Chili with a fantastic lap ahead of Neil; Xaus was fourth, sandwiched between the two Suzukis of Lavilla in third and Reynolds. Xaus spoiled the party festivities for his team-mate with a win in race 1, but the British rider was crowned champion with his runner-up place. Chili was a superb third. Hodgson wasn't going to allow Xaus to get the better of him in race 2 and just edged out his rival for the win, while Lavilla came home in third place. Corser showed a few signs of being competitive with sixth place in the first race for Petronas.

RACES Imola (ITA) • 28/09/03

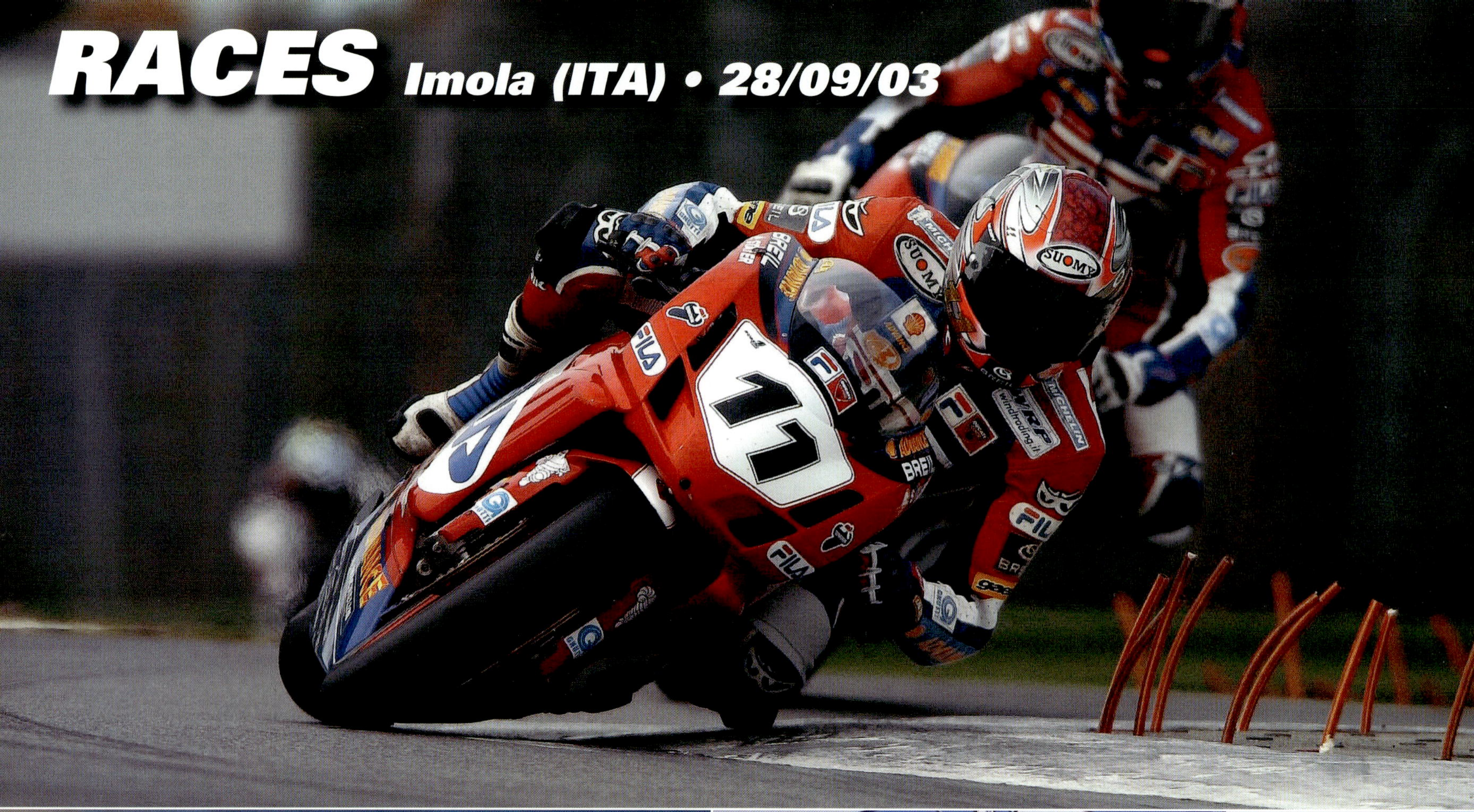

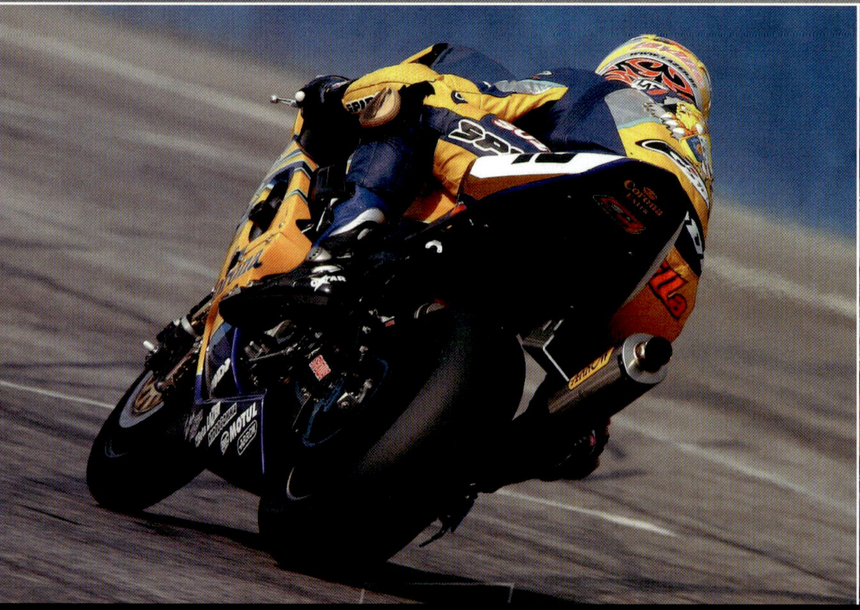

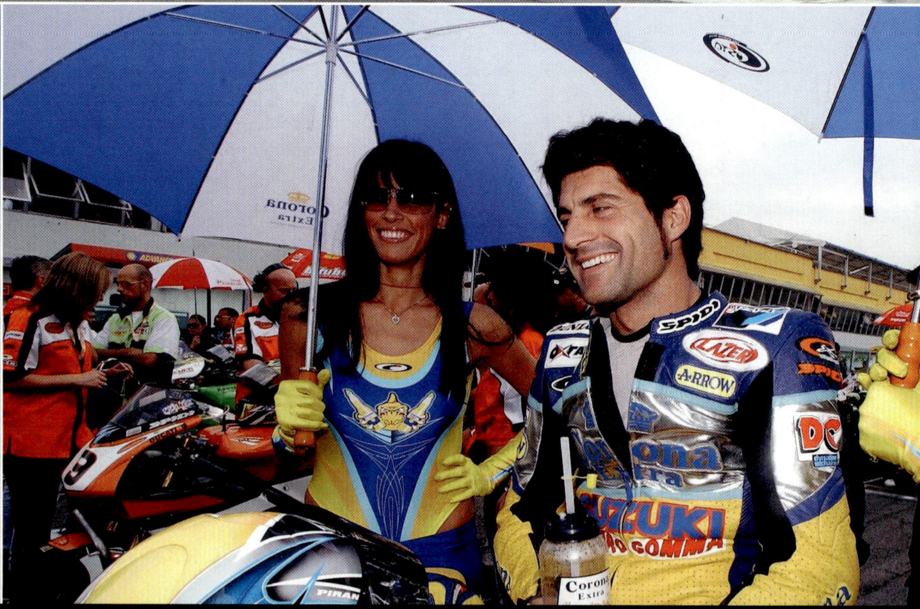

the race

There was none of the emotion of the 2002 race when Bayliss and Edwards clashed for the title but Imola always offers a superb spectacle. Right from the start of Friday qualifying it was clear that Xaus was in superb form and the Spaniard lined up on the grid ahead of a surprising Laconi and team-mate Hodgson. Corser (Petronas) was sixth behind Chili. But Xaus really pulled out all the stops on Sunday when he scored a brilliant double win, beating his team-mate who finished runner-up in race 1 and then fourth in race 2 after a mistake at the Piratella. Laconi with the Ducati NCR and Lavilla with the Suzuki Alstare were the other protagonists of the Imola round, while Corser twice finished seventh with the Petronas.

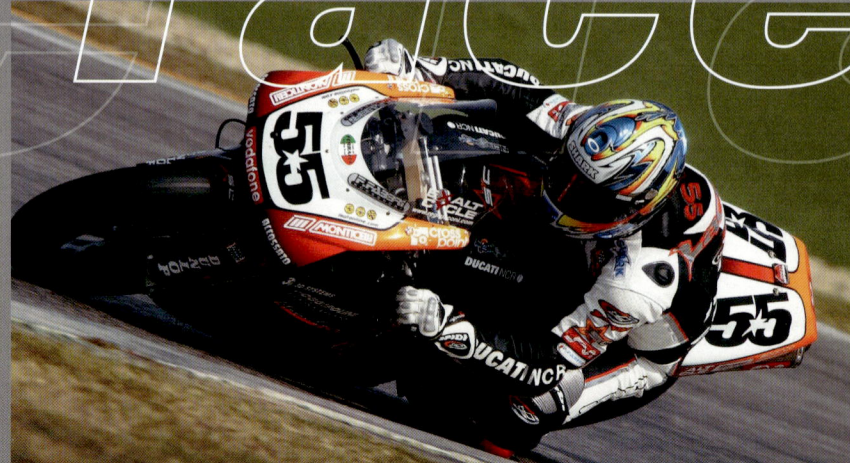

RACES Magny Cours (FRA) • 19/10/03

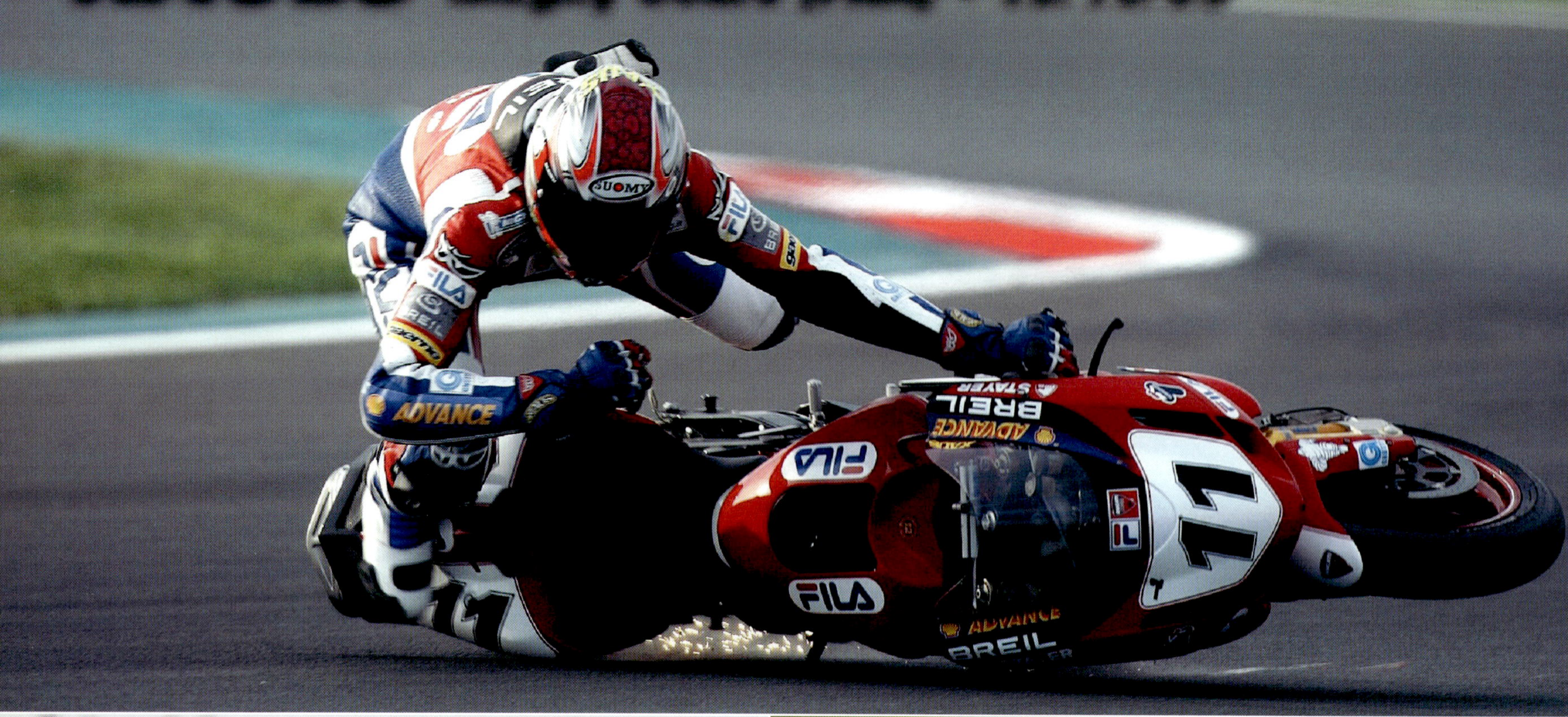

the race

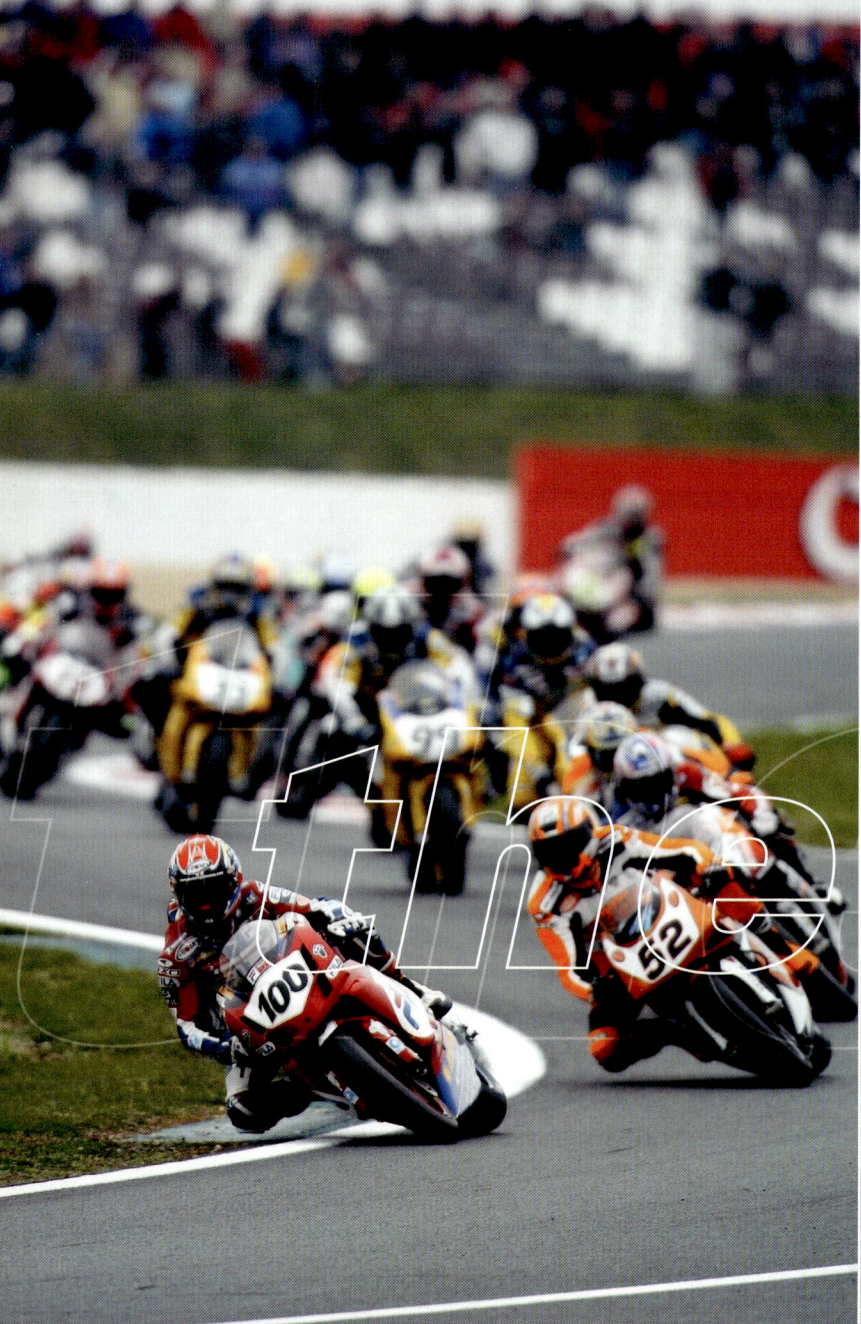

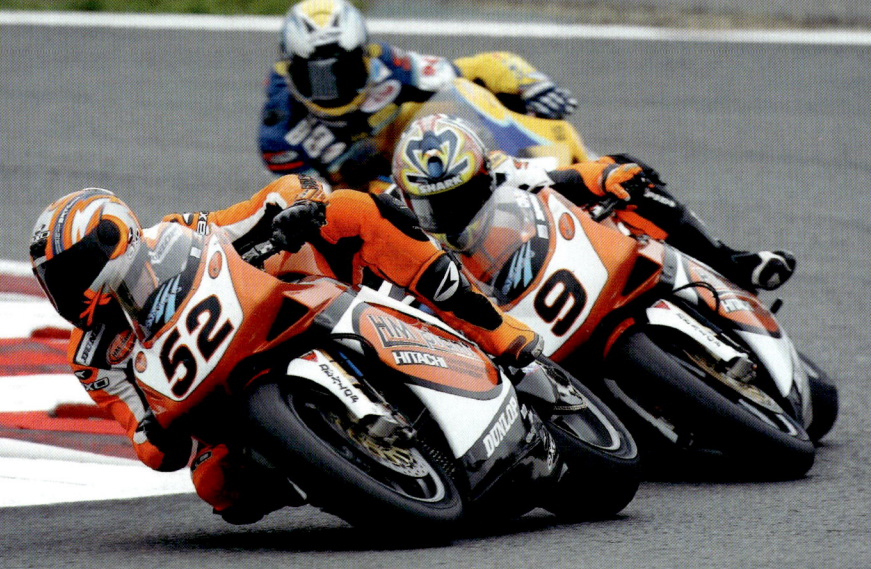

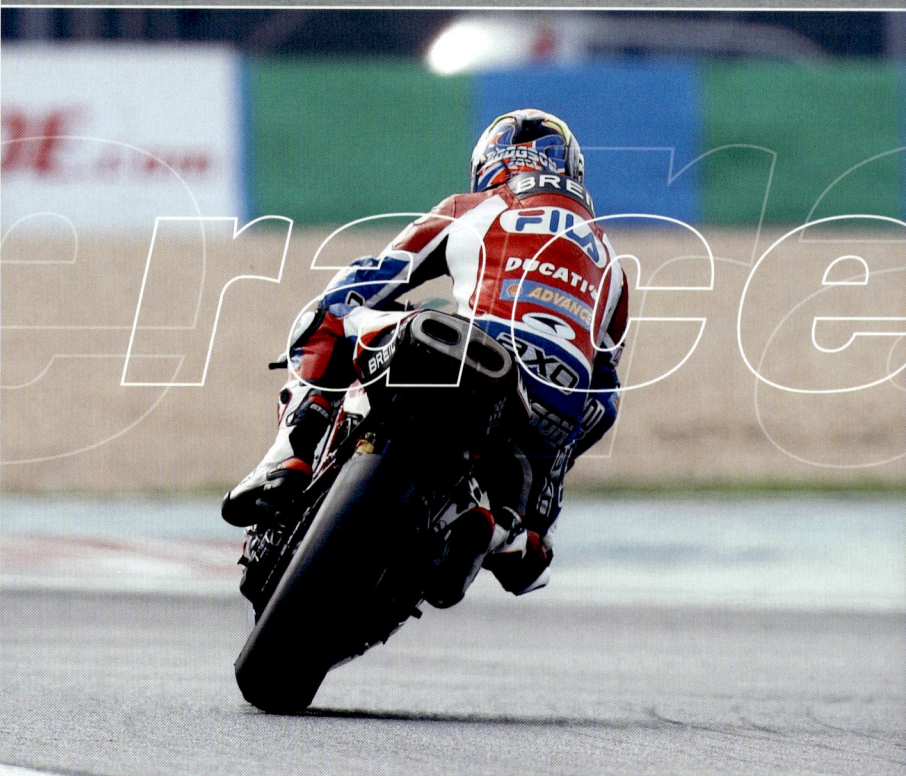

Victory in the final round of the 2003 world championship was a private affair between the two factory Ducati riders. In qualifying, it was James Toseland, Ducati Corse's 2004 factory rider, who set pole from Hodgson, Laconi and Xaus (basically Ducati's present and future line-up) but in the race the 2003 world champion and his team-mate simply powered away from the rest. In race 1 Hodgson and Xaus slugged it out for the win and at the flag it was the British rider who clinched it; third

was Chris Walker who finished ahead of Lavilla (Suzuki). In race 2 an error by Hodgson opened the door for Xaus who won by more than ten seconds from HM Plant's British duo Toseland and Walker in that order. Lavilla (Suzuki) finished fourth again, while Corser crashed his Petronas on the warm-up lap!

FUTURE

e future

TOWARDS THE FUTURE

Every revolution throws up a series of questions over its eventual outcome; on the other hand there are also positive signs that can give us some indications about the future. With the introduction of the new 1000 cc four-cylinder regulations from 2004 onwards, Superbike is not immune to this rule; and while the international bike shows at the end of 2003 have highlighted the importance of the new sports bikes from Japan and Italy, let us analyse the possible starting-points for a rosy future.

In 2003 various national championships had already introduced new norms allowing in the 1000cc four-cylinder bikes in view of the new world championship regulations. These included the United States, Britain, Japan, Italy and Germany. It is not always possible to analyse the performance of the 1000cc bikes in relation to the 'queen' of Superbike, Ducati, but in certain cases it is possible to make a series of projections. In the domestic championships, which are excellent but far from world standard,

the four-cylinder Japanese bikes and Suzuki in particular attempted to contrast the domination of Ducati, which was directly or indirectly present through dealer teams. That is why their success is important, as is the participation of 'wild-card' riders of the calibre of Watanabe, Mladin, Iannuzzo or Kagayama. What counts even more however is the performance of 'private' teams that, thanks to competitive bikes, can compete with factory or factory-supported teams. This observation is also valid for the numerous 'private' Ducati bikes that managed to win virtually everywhere. One of the countries where the Italian manufacturer is not officially present is Japan, which in 2003 saw the domination of the Suzuki GSX-R 1000, winner with Keiichi Kitagawa and second with outgoing champion Atsushi Watanabe. The championship also saw considerable progress made by the Honda CBR 954 RR of Tsujimura. The same can be said about Germany, where expert Andreas Meklau, Ducati's sole representa-

TOWARDS THE FUTURE

tive, could only win one round in the 16-race calendar. The German title went to a talented youngster who has already raced in the world championship: 22 year-old Stefan Nebel, winner with a Suzuki GSX-R 1000, which was also ridden by Italian Markus Wegscheider. Two significant wins were also obtained by Michael Schulten with the promising Honda CBR. Victory in Britain went to Ducati, where Shane Byrne (winner of two world championship races) got the better of some stiff opposition led by veteran John Reynolds with the Rizla Suzuki GSX-R,

which also appeared in several WSBK rounds. Japan's Yu-rio Kagayama was unfortunate to be sidelined by a nasty crash after he had begun to win races, while the Yamahas were disappointing, with the new R1 model yet to make its debut. Staying in Europe, Italy saw one win for the Yamaha R1 of the former 125 cc world champion Alessandro Gramigni, a victory that was then overturned, one for the Suzuki of Vittorio Iannuzzo and two for Ducati with Lucio Pedercini. Victory in the fifth round went to Mauro Sanchini (who also picked up Gramigni's points) with the

'old' Kawasaki ZX-R 750, allowing the Team Bertocchi rider to clinch the Italian Superbike title. Australian Mat Mladin clinched the important American AMA Superbike title with a Suzuki GSX-R 1000 that powered him to ten wins, while team-mate Yates was runner-up. Kurtis Roberts, Ben Bostrom and Miguel DuHamel with the Honda VTR (RC 51) had to settle for third, fourth and fifth respectively. Ducati was troubled by rider problems, while a crash brought a halt to Eric Bostrom's season with the Kawasaki ZX-R 750, boosted to 800cc.

sbk his

The World Superbike Championship got underway in 1988 after its early years in the United States and Australia. Nine rounds were organised in the first year, six in Europe and the others in Japan, Australia and New Zealand. The bikes were production-based with several important modifications, a rule aimed at attracting large numbers of 'private' riders. The first World Superbike champion was American Fred Merkel, who on a Team Rumi Honda VFR, saw off the surprising challenge from ex-motocross rider Fabrizio Pirovano (Yamaha FZR), whose wins included the one at the prestigious Le Mans circuit. The two Bimota YB of Davide Tardozzi, the first-ever winner of a World Superbike race at Donington and Stephane Mertens, as well as the Ducati 851 of Marco Lucchinelli, the first winner of a World Superbike round (Donington was decided on aggregate results), suffered numerous problems, which allowed the American to take the title. His good nature and vague resemblance to the actor Robert Redford allowed Merkel (and as a result Superbike) to make a name for himself outside the motorcycle racing sphere. In this season, a certain Mick Doohan on a Yamaha won races at Sugo (Japan) and Oran Park (Australia). In 1989 the calendar was increased to eleven rounds with the addition of a double-header in the USA and Canada. This was an important addition because in North America Superbike had seen the rise of many riders who then made their name in GP racing throughout Europe: Wayne Rainey, AMA champion in 1983 and 1987, Fred Merkel, Kevin Schwantz and John Kocinski. Despite the championship promoters going bankrupt, Superbike showed it had major potential and constantly attracted large crowds. Honda entered the scene with the RC30, a competitive version of its four-cylinder 750, with which Fred Merkel won a second world title, beating Stephane Mertens, who was on a similar bike. The Ducati 851 showed a major improvement over the previous year and this season was raced by the expert and gutsy Fren-

Fred Merkel - Honda - 1988

chman Raymond Roche, together with Baldassarre Monti. Roche, who had previously raced 250, 350 and 500 GP bikes as well as in Endurance) helped to develop the twin-cylinder machine from Bologna, which was destined for a great future. While Fabrizio Pirovano had another excellent season, the man to watch was Giancarlo Falappa who won three races on a competitive Bimota. 1990 saw the arrival of the Flammini Group as promoters and they soon revived the category. A major contribution to this came from the victory of Ducati thanks to the superb performances of Roche, who won the championship from the two Honda riders, Merkel and Mertens. American Doug Polen, who was only scheduled by Ducati to take part in a few races and then to concentrate on the American series, dominated the opening round of the 1991 championship. Doug, riding a Fast by Ferracci Ducati, would instead remain in the series, win-

ning 17 out of the 26 races, including six double wins! Despite a superb second half of the season, Roche was unable to do anything against the American and settled for the runner-up slot. Stephane Mertens also went well now that he had switched to a Ducati, and so did Rob Phillis, who was turning the Kawasaki into force to be reckoned with. Polen was still hungry for the wins however and he repeated his triumph in 1992, taking a second successive title despite stiff opposition from Roche, who was determined to leave the series on a high note. The arrival of Kiwi Aaron Slight alongside Phillis in the Kawasaki team marked another step forward for the Japanese manufacturer, while Falappa (Ducati) and Pirovano (Yamaha) were also competitive. The 1993 season saw the arrival of another American, Scott Russell. Thanks to the Muzzy team, the rider from Georgia had already taken part in a few WSBK races, but he was

Doug Polen - Ducati - 1991

aymond Roche - Ducati - 1990

Scott Russel - Kawasaki - 1993

Troy Corser - Ducati - 1996

John Kocinski - Honda - 1997

now involved full-time. The results were surprising to say the least and the rider with the redskin motif on his helmet took the world title from Giancarlo Falappa and Carl Fogarty on Ducatis. Slight finished third, followed by Pirovano in his last season on a Yamaha before moving to Ducati. The following year Honda returned to WSBK in a big way with the splendid RC45, which was raced by the talented New Zealander Aaron Slight. The Castrol Honda rider was one of the stars of the 1994 season, battling against Carl Fogarty, who took the Ducati 916 to its debut, and the outgoing champion Scott Russell. The American powered into an early championship lead, but from Spain onwards was then overhauled by Fogarty. Slight also had a brief spell at the top but his points in Britain were allowed and then taken away again due to a case of illegal fuel. The situation was complicated but Fogarty continued to aim for the title, which he won with a text-book race at Phillip Island against Russell and Slight. No one could ever have imagined at the time that this would be the start of an incredible series of titles that 'Foggy' would go on to win for Ducati. The Bri-

tish rider repeated his triumph in 1995, the season in which the Italian manufacturer picked up its 100th WSBK win (in Austria), and which saw the emergence of the talented young Australian Troy Corser, winner of the AMA title. The following year Fogarty decided to switch to Honda and in response Ducati signed none other than John Kocinski. The American joined the team run by Virginio Ferrari, who was one of the few people capable of managing the notoriously difficult American. Troy Corser was in a separately-run factory Ducati squad, while Fogarty's team-mate was Sli-

ght. These four riders were still in with a chance of taking the title as the season drew to a close, but the 1996 crown eventually went to the Australian after a double win at Albacete and a class performance on his home circuit. World Superbike was shaken up again in 1997 when Fogarty and Kocinski swapped teams and Corser moved to GP racing, while Russell returned with Yamaha. Only Fogarty and Kocinski were in with a chance of winning however and in the end the title went to the American. Another of the stars of the season was Pierfrancesco Chili with a privately-run Du-

Carl Fogarty - Ducati - 1998

Colin Edwards - Honda - 2000

cati. In 1998 the 23 year-old Japanese rider Noriyuki Haga burst onto the scene and, at least in the early rounds, proved to be tough opposition for Fogarty, who went on to conquer a third Riders' title. Unfortunately Haga crashed at Monza and the main opposition now became Colin Edwards, who was fast emerging for Castrol Honda after switching from Yamaha. Corser was also back on the pace, but it was Fogarty who finished the strongest after his difficult early part of the season. At the mid-point Aaron Slight also became a candidate for the title, but in the end he could only finish runner-up as Fogarty took his third WSBK crown. Chili also had another good season with some superb performances on a Ducati. Carl Fogarty became the first rider to win four WSBK titles in 1999 on the Ducati 996. His domination was never in doubt and the British rider outdistanced second-placed men Colin Edwards (Honda) and Troy Corser (Ducati) by 130 points. Aaron Slight (Honda) and Akira Yanagawa (Kawasaki) also had good seasons. The number of world championship victories for 'Foggy' could have been higher had it not been for a crash at the start of 2000 which first forced him to miss the rest of the season and then to retire from racing. It was tough blow for Superbike and for Ducati. The title went to Colin Edwards on the brand-new Honda VTR, five years after he had arrived in Superbike with Yamaha and three years after he had switched to Honda. Haga had looked to be favourite to win the title, but a rather murky question of doping ruined his season. Troy Bayliss exploded onto the scene after being drafted into Ducati from the AMA championship and the Australian surprisingly finished sixth overall. And still on the subject of Australians, Corser won some races in his debut season with Aprilia. The 2001 season saw a new breed of hero emerge as Bayliss took the title, thanks also to a superbly competitive Ducati 998. His chief rival was again Edwards, who headed home his fellow-American Ben Bostrom (Ducati) in the championship standings. Corser failed to improve with the Aprilia, while Britain's Neil Hodgson had a positive season on a private Ducati. The 2002

championship was again characterised by the duel between Bayliss and Edwards and their titanic battle went right down to the wire at the Imola finale. Just 11 points separated the two as the American took the crown. Colin Edwards and Troy Bayliss would meet up again the following year in MotoGP. Third place went to Neil Hodgson who was signed by the factory Ducati squad for the 2003 season.

Troy Bayliss - Ducati - 2001

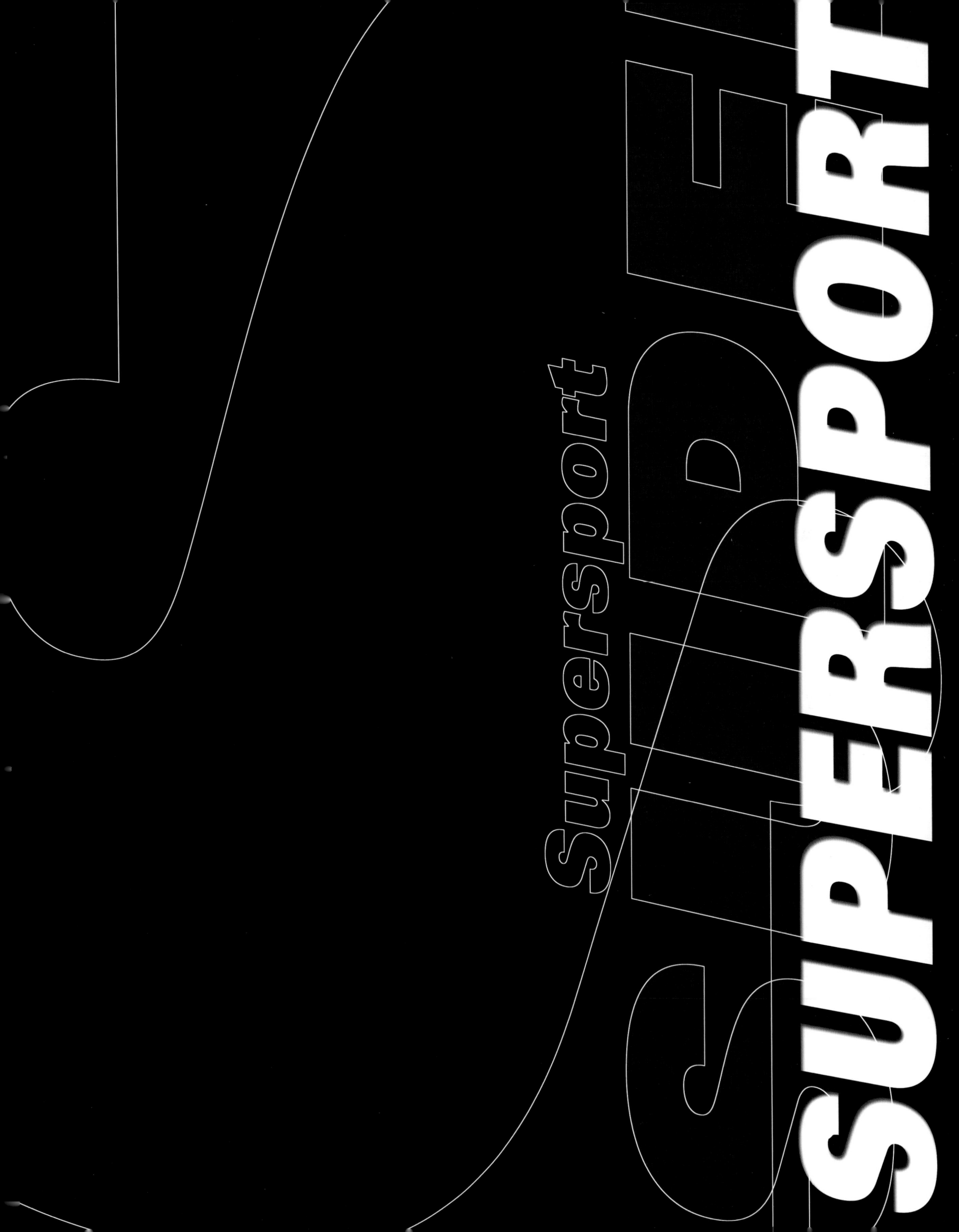

With the win in Assen by team-mate Karl Muggeridge, Chris Vermeulen had to wait until Imola to be mathematically sure of winning the world title, but the talented youngster had more or less clinched it a couple of races before. The win by the Australian, whom Honda have been keeping an eye on for some time, has maybe opened up a new era in Supersport. In fact, after seeing a number of experienced riders take the title over the years, the 600 class this season rewarded a promising young rider, who accomplished his 'mission' in preparation for the World Superbike championship. Vermeulen, in his third full season in Supersport, had never won a race before this year, but soon made up for this by winning four times, at Phillip Island, Monza, Oschersleben and Silverstone. He was certainly helped by an ultra-competitive and fantastic Honda CBR600 prepared by Dutch team, Ten Kate, but judging by the results of his Honda colleagues, a lot of his success was down to the Australian himself. The Vermeulen story began in 1998 when he made his debut in the Australian 250cc championship, finishing eighth. That same year Chris also raced in 750 (similar to Superbike) and in one of the races caught the eye of the late Barry Sheene. The man himself was so impressed with Vermeulen that he organised a trip for him to Britain, where he took part in Superstock. The young Australian soon overcame all the difficulties of living far away from home

EN

ampion

CHRIS VERMEULEN

and started to appear on the results sheets. In 2000 he was given a ride in the World Supersport championship by Castrol Honda and finished sixth at Assen, a result that was confirmed with tenth place in the final round in Britain. Much was expected of Vermeulen the following year but the results were disappointing, and the season was marked by a number of crashes and the odd finish. In 2002 things changed: two pole positions, a second place at Monza, third at Imola and seventh overall. All this was happening for Chris at just 20 years of age and Honda did the right thing by promoting him in 2003 from the Van-zon satellite team to the main Ten Kate outfit, which gave him a virtually unbeatable version of the new CBR600RR. The largest motorcycle manufacturer in the world has created another world champion and 21 year-old Vermeulen (born on June 19, 1982 in Brisbane, Australia) seems destined for a glorious career with the Japanese company: next year he will switch to Superbike with the new Honda and then we will truly see what he is capable of.

#7 Chris Vermeulen

SUPERSPORT
WORLD CHAMPIONSHIP

worldsb

World
Champion
2003

Ten Kate

WSS RIDERS

While Chris Vermeulen dominated the Supersport championship (200 points, four wins, three pole positions), there were several riders who gave him a tough time at the front. These included stalwart Stephane Chambon, who at 38 years of age continues to be one of the stars of the category. Although not one of the favourites, Team Alstare's French rider is so much in sync with the Suzuki GSX-R 600 that he was always at the front and he finished runner-up, with one win at Brands Hatch to his credit. Chambon did better that his team-mate Katsuaki Fujiwara, who after winning the Valencia opener, alternated the good with the bad and in the end he was sidelined with a crash. The Japanese rider, runner-up the previous year, finished fifth overall. A lot was expected of Yamaha but the Japanese manufacturer failed to pick up many good results, despite Jurgen van den Goorbergh finishing an excellent third overall. In his first season with four-

stroke machinery, the 33 year-old Dutchman from Breda set one pole position and scored six podiums for the Belgarda team. These positive results were not repeated by his young team-mate Simone Sanna, who at least demonstrated his potential at Misano with pole position. One win for Yamaha did come from German Christian Kellner, but his performances did not live up to his past results, and the same can be said of team-mate Jorg Teuchert, who could only finish tenth.

Eighth place went to Alessio Corradi, the 27 year-old rider for the Italian Spadaro Team, who had a good season. He finished on the podium at Valencia and was fifth at Silverstone. The most competitive and eagerly-awaited bike was the Honda CBR 600 RR, which as well as those of Vermeulen, also scored three wins in the hands of his team-mate, 29 year-old Karl Muggeridge. The Australian appeared to be destined for a brilliant career but had been very disappointing until the three

wins in the final part of the season. Other disappointing riders were Charpentier, who showed what he was capable of during the second half of the season, moving up to seventh overall, Parkes (possibly the best rider of the bunch judging by the bike's potential), MacPherson and Daemen. The real disappointment of the season however was Kawasaki, which despite two riders of the calibre of reigning champion Fabien Foret and the quick Spaniard, Pere Riba, was unable to add to its single victory at Misano by the Frenchman. Foret's switch from the German to the French team and a lack of development on the competitive ZX-6RR did not help matters for the two riders, who are amongst the best around in Supersport. After wins for four different manufacturers in 2003, next year's Supersport championship will see the arrival of Ducati and the return of the Italo-Japanese battle for supremacy.

RACES
Valencia (ESP) • 02/03/03

The Supersport championship got underway without two of its stalwarts, Casoli and Whitham, who had decided to retire. At Valencia, the bike with the highest expectations, the Honda CBR-RR, was defeated by the Suzuki of Katsuaki Fujiwara who finished more than 4 seconds ahead of Vermeulen. A surprise third was Corradi (Team Italia-Yamaha), who got the better of Cogan (Honda) and former champion Teuchert. The Kawasakis of Foret and Riba were both disappointing.

RACES *Phillip Island (AUS) • 30/03/03*

C hris Vermeulen was on pole for his home race with the most competitive bike around, the Honda CBR-RR, ahead of Chambon, Fujiwara and Foret; and it was the young Australian who dominated the race, despite some tough early opposition from the Japanese rider. Third place went to Holland's van den Goorbergh after a superb recovery. After two races Vermeulen and Fujiwara were equal on points.

RACES Sugo (JPN) • 27/04/03

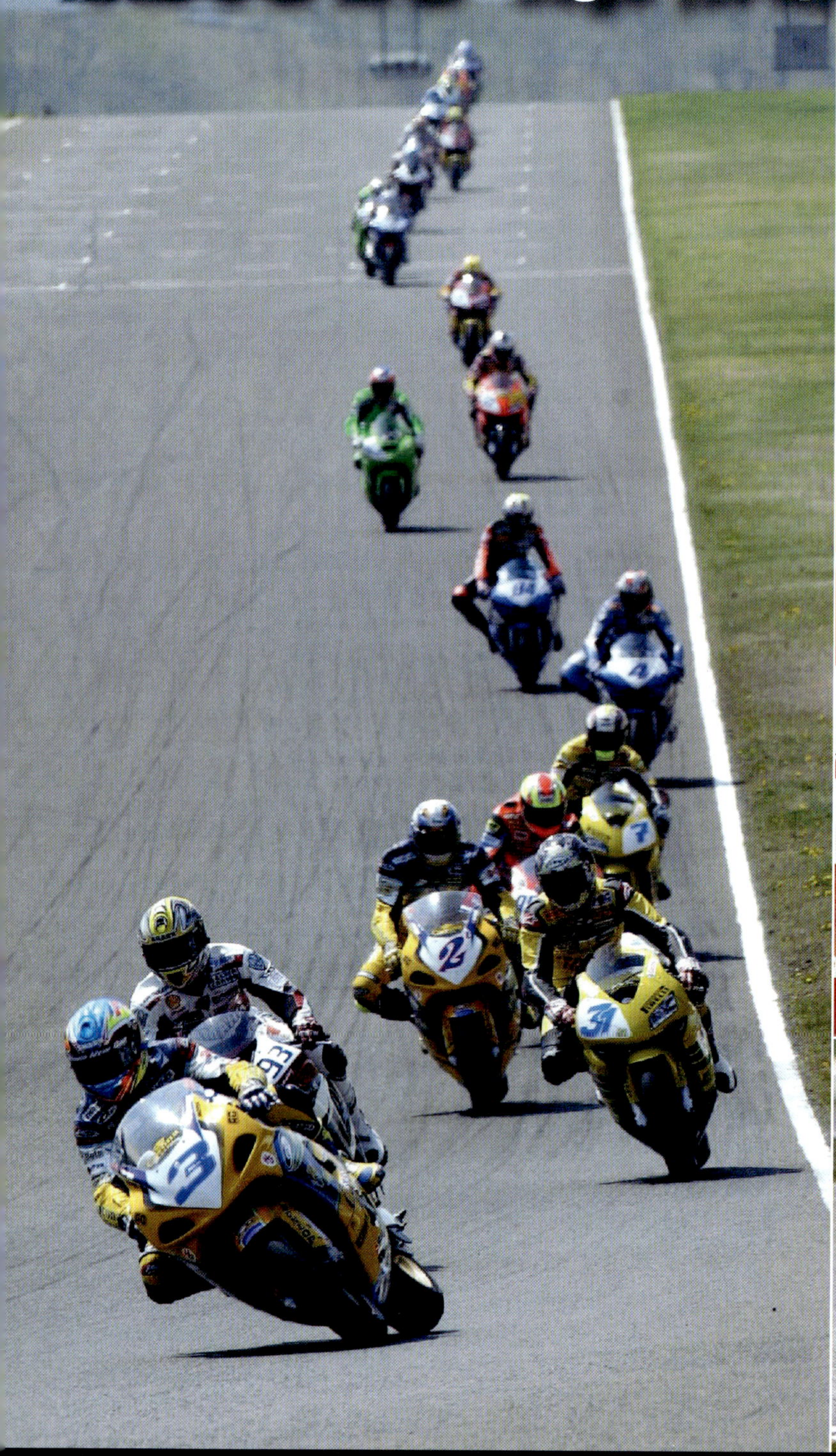

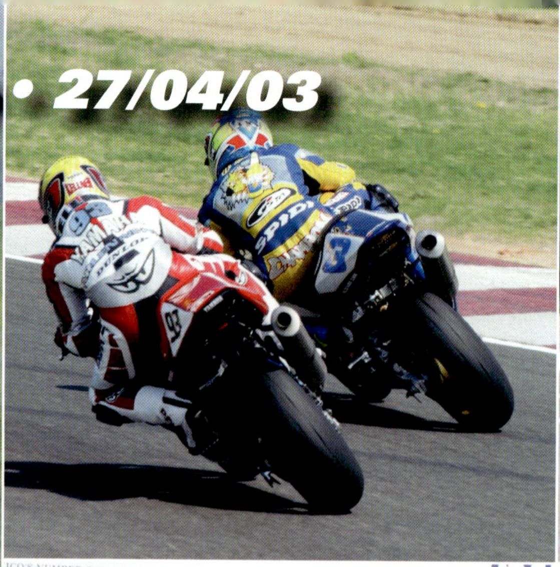

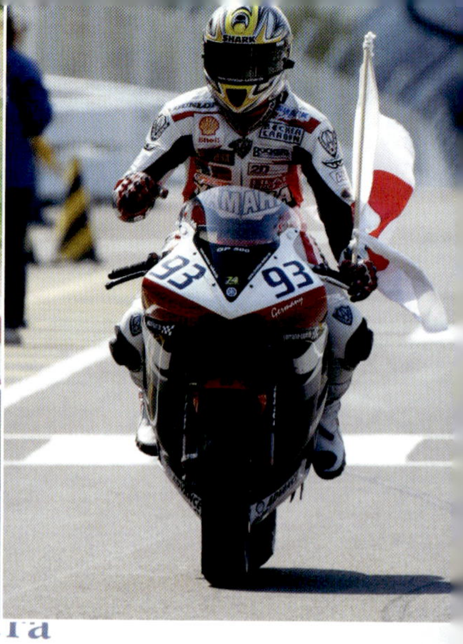

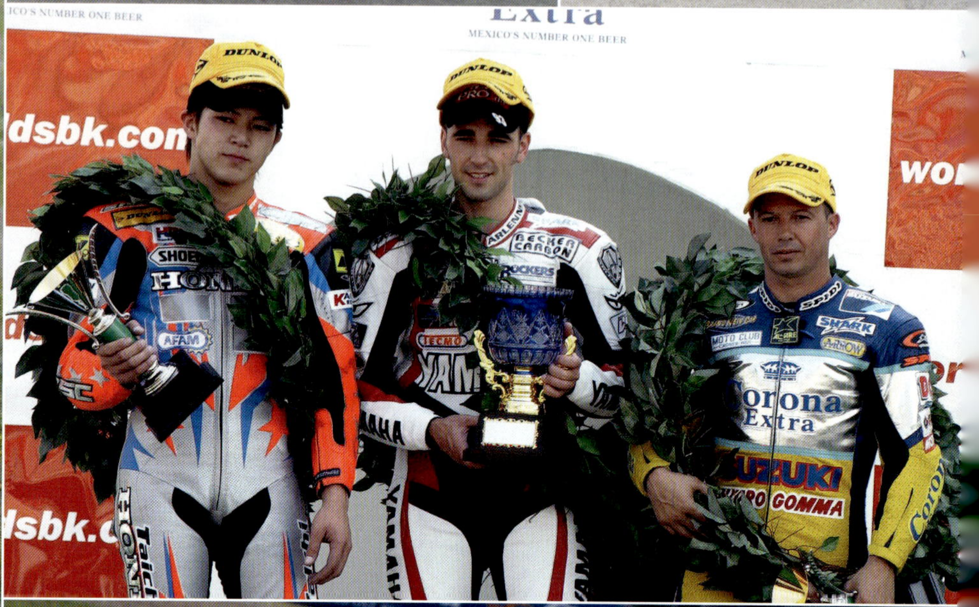

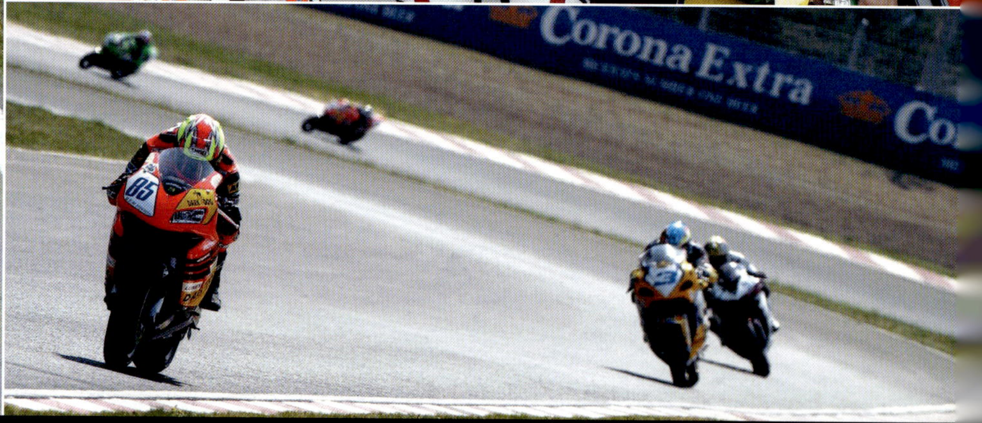

the race

Fujiwara set an unofficial track record in qualifying for his home race from team-mate Chambon. But it was the surprising Yamaha of Christian Kellner who went on to win from the BKM Honda of wild-card Kiyonari and the Suzuki of Chambon. Fujiwara crashed while Vermeulen, fifth behind Tekkin Kayo (Yamaha-Belgarda), was now out in front in the points table.

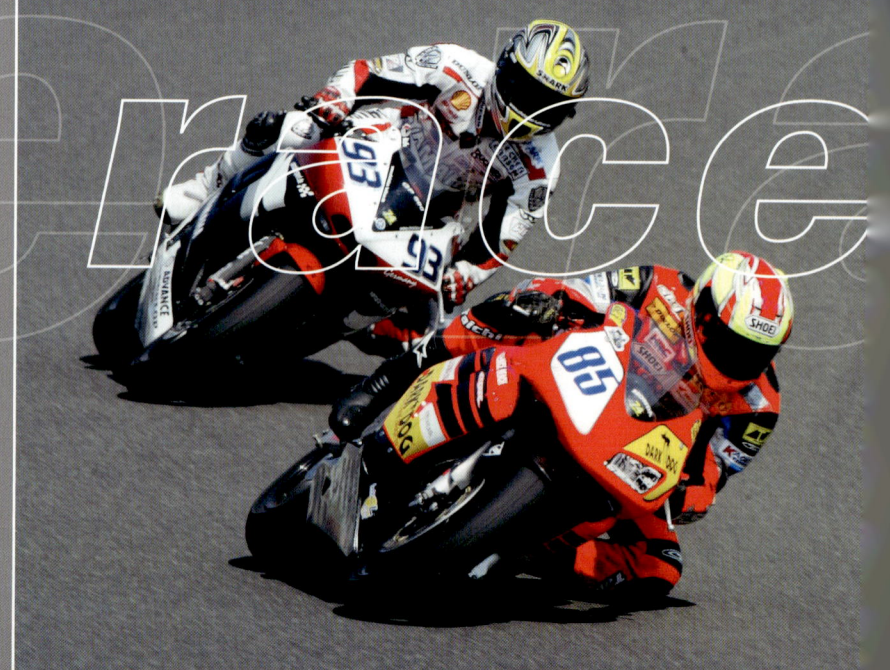

A rejuvenated Muggeridge was on pole ahead of Vermeulen, who crashed in practice, Riba (Kawasaki) and Fujiwara, while the Yamahas were further back. In the race the championship leader annihilated the rest of the field with a series of record laps to finish nine seconds ahead of van den Goorbergh; MacPherson and Chambon were further back, while Muggeridge was forced to retire with a clutch problem. After four rounds Vermeulen had a 29 point lead over Fujiwara and 30 over van den Goorbergh.

RACES Oschersleben (GER) • 01/06/03

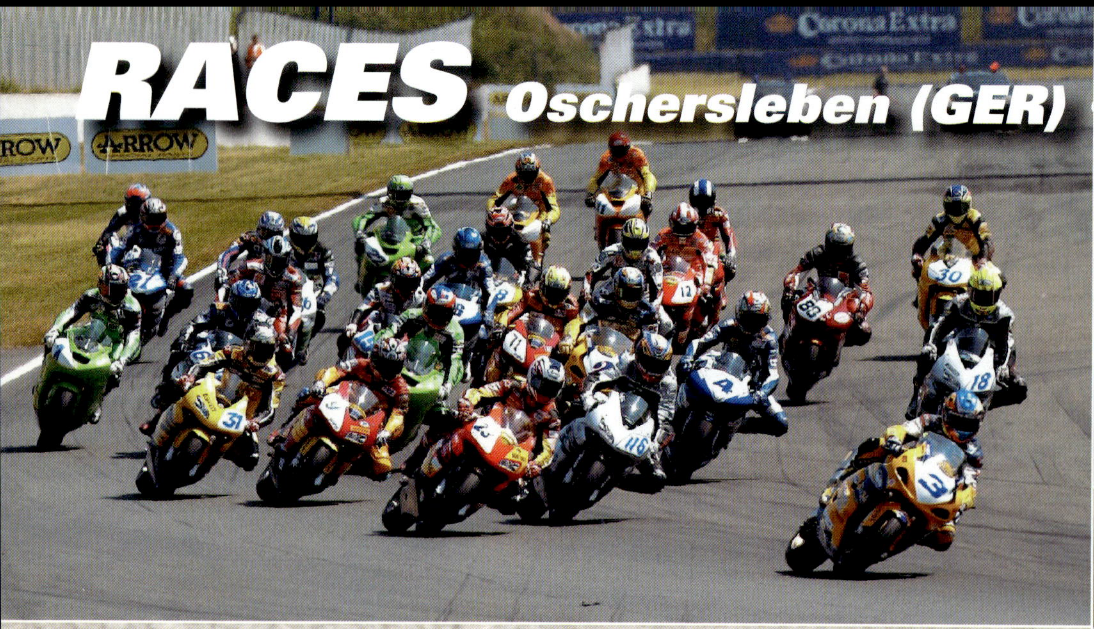

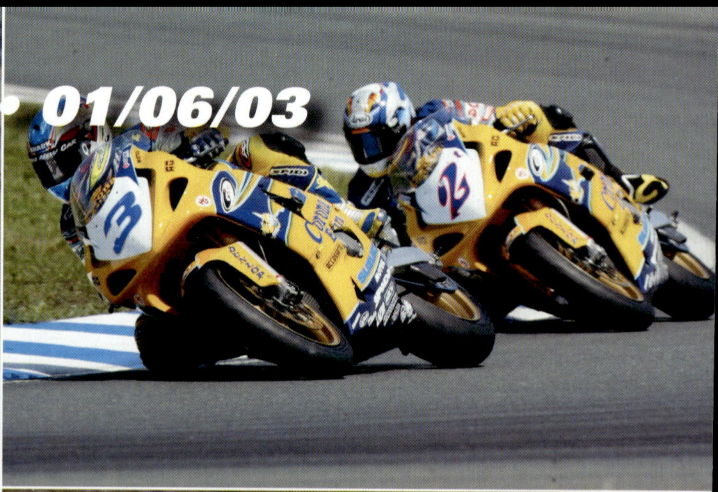

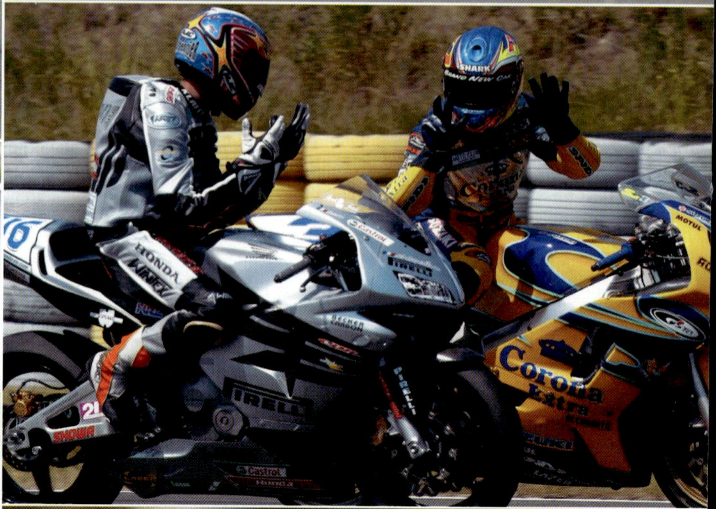

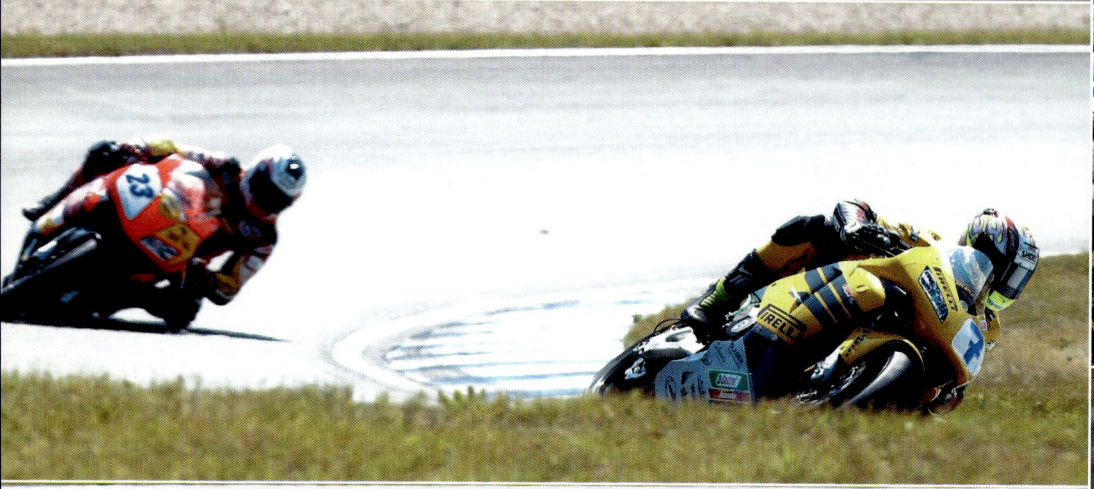

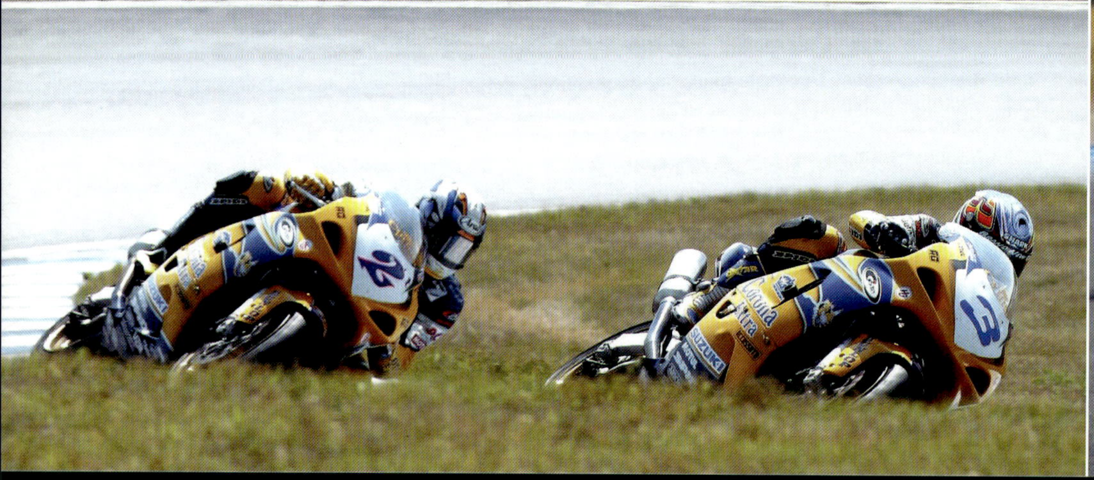

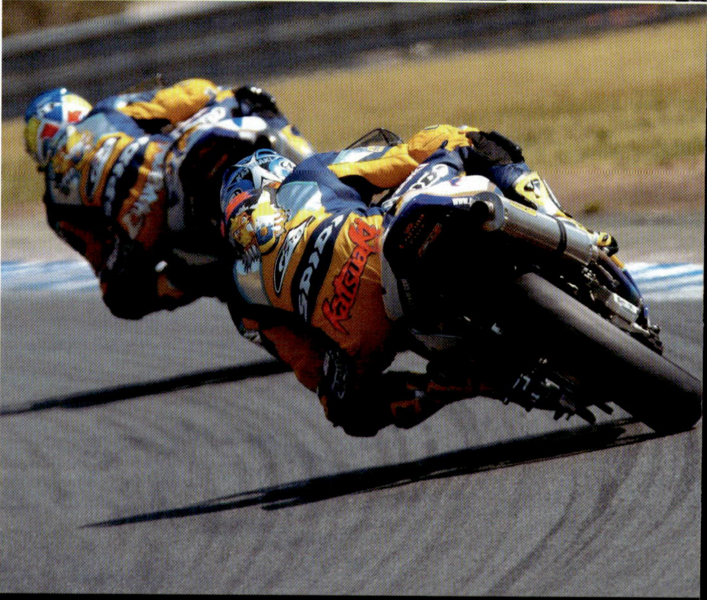

Another pole position for Muggeridge, ahead of Vermeulen, Chambon and Charpentier. Things were back to normal in the race with the third win in five rounds for Vermeulen, who took his points lead to 38. The surprise of the day was Broc Parkes who caught up to the leader but then dropped to fifth place when his tyres deteriorated. The runner-up slot went to Chambon ahead of Fuijwara who held on to second place in the championship.

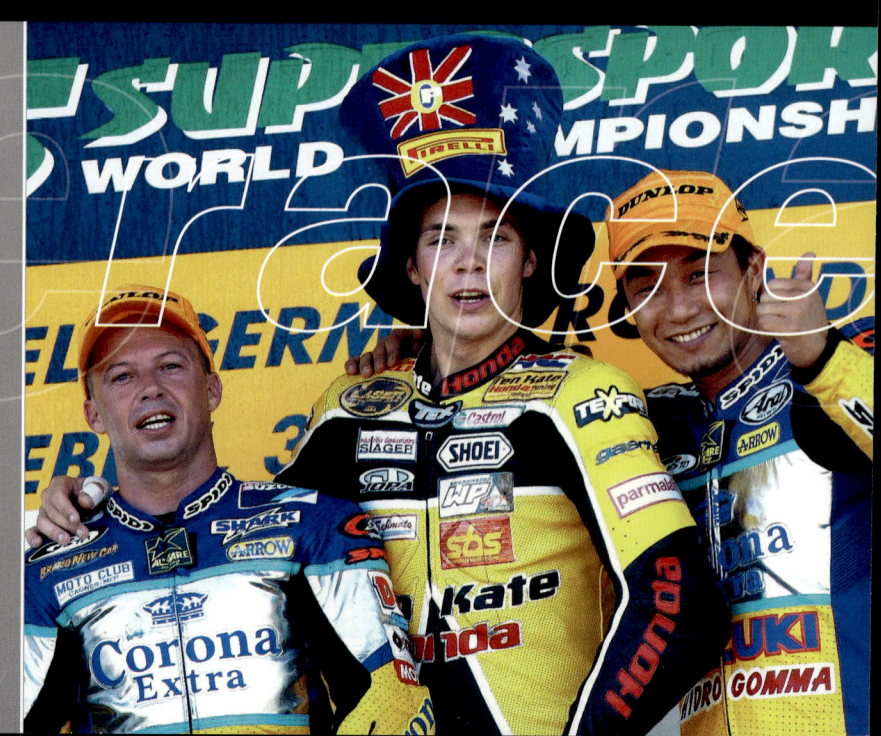

RACES *Silverstone (GBR) • 15/06/03*

Two years after its last pole position, a Yamaha was on the top of the qualifying timesheets thanks to Van der Goorbergh. Vermeulen could only manage sixth behind Chambon, Fuijwara, Sanna and Corradi. It was all an illusion however as young Chris went on to win, way ahead of van den Goorbergh, Muggeridge, Frenchman Van den Bosch and Corradi.

SILVERSTONE
13, 14, 15 JUNE 2003

RACES
Misano (RSM) • 22/06/03

Young Italian Yamaha-Belgarda rider Simone Sanna set a fantastic pole position ahead of van den Goorbergh. The race was an exciting one, starting with a crash for Vermeulen, while van den Goorbergh retired with an engine problem. Fujiwara powered into the lead but he was unable to hold off Fabien Foret (Kawasaki), who went on to win from the Japanese rider and Australian Broc Parkes.

RACES *Brands Hatch • (EUR) 27/07/03*

Chambon set pole position at Brands Hatch ahead of a rejuvenated Foret; but it was the Suzuki GSX-R rider who scored a superb solitary win as the Frenchman headed home van den Goorbergh by seven seconds. Third went to Charpentier (Honda Klaffi), while Vermeulen could only manage sixth. The Australian however still led the championship by 37 points from van den Goorbergh.

RACES Assen (NED) · 07/09/03

Supersport arrived at Assen, Netherlands, the home circuit of the Ten Kate team that was dominating the championship; and it was their two riders who set the pace. Muggeridge was proving to be a much-improved rider in the last few races and he scored a surprise win, his first of the season from Vermeulen by just 263/1000ths of a second. Third was Fuijwara, followed by Chambon, who was now ahead of van den Goorbergh in the standings after the Dutchman crashed.

Muggeridge set a cracking pace in qualifying and lined up on pole ahead of Chambon, Vermeulen and Charpentier. The race saw a superb battle between the two Ten Kate riders, and the win went to Muggeridge in a sprint finish to the line with Vermeulen, who mathematically clinched the 2003 title. Van den Goorbergh again finished on the podium with third place.

RACES

the race

The Magny-Cours circuit saw one of the most monotonous races of the season as Karl Muggeridge powered to his third win on the run after starting from pole. 2003 world champion Chris Vermeulen was runner-up, three and a half seconds behind. Van den Goorbergh finished third after a superb recovery that saw him overtake local rider Charpentier in the final stages of the race. Chambon finished fifth to hold on to second place in the overall standings.

Riders Standing

1	C. Vermeulen	(AUS)	Honda	201
2	S. Chambon	(FRA)	Suzuki	137
3	J. Vd Goorbergh	(NED)	Yamaha	136
4	K. Muggeridge	(AUS)	Honda	134
5	K. Fujiwara	(JPN)	Suzuki	119
6	C. Kellner	(GER)	Yamaha	90
7	S. Charpentier	(FRA)	Honda	72
8	A. Corradi	(ITA)	Yamaha	68
9	F. Foret	(FRA)	Kawasaki	64
10	J. Teuchert	(GER)	Yamaha	60
11	P. Riba	(ESP)	Kawasaki	59
12	C. Cogan	(FRA)	Honda	51
13	B. Parkes	(AUS)	Honda	47
14	I. MacPherson	(GBR)	Honda	31
15	G. Nannelli	(ITA)	Yamaha	31
16	M. Lagrive	(FRA)	Yamaha	31
17	S. Sanna	(ITA)	Yamaha	29
18	W. Daemen	(BEL)	Honda	26
19	R. Ulm	(AUT)	Honda	26
20	T. Kayo	(JPN)	Yamaha	22
21	R. Kiyonari	(JPN)	Honda	20
22	T. Vd Bosch	(FRA)	Yamaha	13
23	K. Curtain	(AUS)	Yamaha	11
24	B. Veneman	(NED)	Honda	11
25	D. Thomas	(AUS)	Honda	9
26	A. Carlacci	(ITA)	Yamaha	7
27	S. Cruciani	(ITA)	Kawasaki	6
28	M. Schulten	(GER)	Honda	5
29	J. Da Costa	(FRA)	Kawasaki	4
30	M. Laverty	(ITA)	Honda	4
31	T. Sykes	(GBR)	Yamaha	4
32	T. Tsujimura	(JPN)	Honda	4
33	A. Polita	(ITA)	Yamaha	4
34	J. Hanson	(SWE)	Honda	2
35	L. Holon	(FRA)	Yamaha	1
36	I. Goi	(ITA)	Yamaha	1

Bold, sincere and without any respect for formalities: that is the identikit of Michael Fabrizio, the new champion of European Superstock, the promotional category of the Superbike 'circus'. With current 1000cc bikes lapping almost at superbike pace, talented young riders can quickly get to learn the European tracks that they will then encounter in the world championships. The newly-crowned European Superstock champion, Michel Fabrizio, had only really raced outside Italy at Assen before but soon adapted to the new tracks, winning at Monza and Silverstone as well as Misano and Imola, which he knew already. He was backed up by a splendid Suzuki GSX-R 1000, a professional squad like Francesco Batta's Alstare outfit and a manager of the calibre of Fabrizio Pirovano who followed him step by step, trying to contain the occasional over-exuberance of the 19 year-old rider from Rome. The team are hoping that he will mature with age and follow in the footsteps of Vittorio Iannuzzo, who took the title for the team before

him. A worthy rival for Fabrizio was Lorenzo Lanzi of Team Rox, who has been deservedly called up by the factory Ducati squad to race the new 749R in the 2004 World Supersport championship. The 22 year-old from Cesena put together some excellent races, winning four, while at Imola he made a fatal mistake, and in others he was halted by technical problems. The performance of these two riders demonstrates that if well-run, Superstock as well as Supersport are a valid training-ground for Superbike and further proof

of this comes from Iannuzzo in the few SBK rounds he competed in. Third overall went to 2000 and 2001 European Superstock champion James Ellison from Britain, who deserves a shot at Superbike, judging by his win at Brands Hatch and two podiums this year on a Suzuki. The leading group of riders also included Lorenzo Alfonsi, 23 years old from Sesto Fiorentino and rider for the Italian Motorcycling Federation-backed Team Italia-Lorenzini. The Tuscany rider did not win a race but stepped onto the podium three times,

SUPERSTOCK

compensating for the limited competitiveness of the current Yamaha R1 (the situation should change next year with the arrival of the new model) with his gritty determination. The list of Italians continues because the top 10 included six of them. Alfonsi was followed by former European 250 cc champion Riccardo Chiarello (Ducati 999R), who twice finished second with a couple of good performances. Behind him was Gianluca Vizziello, who had an up-and-down season with a few technical problems on his Yamaha and rookie revelation Ilario Dionisi, who set two pole positions with a Team Celani Suzuki. The top 10 was made up of two Spanish riders, Enrique Rocamora and Bernat Martinez, both on Suzukis, who were often amongst the leading groups, and William De Angelis from San Marino who rode the other Team Rox Ducati 999R.

Riders Standing

1	M. Fabrizio	(ITA)	Suzuki	140
2	L. Lanzi	(ITA)	Ducati	137
3	J. Ellison	(GBR)	Suzuki	112
4	L. Alfonsi	(ITA)	Yamaha	98
5	R. Chiarello	(ITA)	Ducati	95
6	G. Vizziello	(ITA)	Yamaha	79
7	I. Dionisi	(ITA)	Suzuki	78
8	E. Rocamora	(ESP)	Suzuki	75
9	B. Martinez	(ESP)	Suzuki	72
10	W. De Angelis	(RSM)	Ducati	50
11	A. Martinez	(ESP)	Suzuki	49
12	A. Velini	(ITA)	Yamaha	40
13	L. Quigley	(GBR)	Suzuki	35
14	J. Laverty	(ITA)	Suzuki	33
15	P. Vanstaen	(FRA)	Suzuki	30
16	J. Hurtado R.	(ESP)	Suzuki	21
17	B. Wilson	(GBR)	Suzuki	15
18	M. Bisconti	(ITA)	Yamaha	15
19	A. Brannetti	(ITA)	Aprilia	11
20	S. Brogan	(GBR)	Suzuki	10
21	B. Wylie	(GBR)	Suzuki	9
22	M. Laverty	(ITA)	Suzuki	9
23	G. Romanelli	(ITA)	Suzuki	7
24	A. Badovini	(ITA)	Ducati	7
25	M. Bottalico	(ITA)	Suzuki	7
26	E. Pasini	(ITA)	Suzuki	4
27	A. Buzzi	(ITA)	Suzuki	4
28	C. Dal Corso	(ITA)	Ducati	4
29	D. Cudlin	(AUS)	Ducati	3
30	G. Dietrich	(FRA)	Suzuki	2
31	G. Scillieri	(ITA)	Yamaha	2
32	K. Reilly	(GBR)	Suzuki	2
33	N. Saelens	(BEL)	Honda	2
34	J. Smrz	(CZE)	Honda	1
35	M. Tonini	(ITA)	Aprilia	1
36	F. De Marco	(ITA)	Yamaha	1

SIDECAR

As always the sidecar championship was a hard-fought affair, with the battle for victory raging between the usual suspects, Abbott, Steinhausen, Klaffenbock and Webster, the top four in 2002. In the end the title went to Steve Webster and Paul Woodhead, the experienced and successful (in particular the former) British pairing. 43 year-old Webster picked up his ninth title win in the category, with a selection of different 'passengers'. Webster and Woodhead, who raced with a Suzuki 1000 powered LCR chassis, also won the title for the second successive year. The 2003 championship began in Spain with a superb win for Webster-Woodhead, 11" ahead of their rivals, while Steinhausen-Hopkinson (Suzuki) retired on the opening lap. The following round at Monza it was the turn of the two British riders to retire, while the win went to the Austrian pairing of Klaus Klaffenbock and Christian Parzer (Yamaha), who moved into the lead of the table. Webster-Woodhead took the win at Oschersleben ahead of the Austrians who held onto their championship lead while Jorg Steinhausen looked to be in diffi-

culty after his second retirement of the year. The finishing order was the same at Silverstone, while at Misano the Anglo-German pairing of Steinhausen-Hopkinson were back on the top of the podium ahead of the surprising Tom Hanks-Phil Briggs (Yamaha). With third place Webster managed to reduce the points gap to Klaffenbock, who finished fourth. The sidecar championship was now turning into a duel between riders of 1000cc four-stroke Yamaha and Suzuki-powered machines. The turning point in the championship came at Brands Hatch, where Webster, as well as

picking up the 33rd pole position of his career (!), took the win from Steinhausen and Klaffenbock and moved into the lead of the title race. With two races over the weekend, Assen looked as if it was going to be the title decider. Webster and Woodhead picked up a double win, while Klaffenbock and Parzer could only manage a second and a third place. After finishing runner-up in race 1, Steinhausen put in a superb performance in the second race, finishing sixth despite having to come into the pits for a quick stop! Unfortunately the German rider now had no chance

SIDECAR

of taking the title as he was more than 50 points behind the leader, Webster. The reigning world champions, Steve Abbott and Jamie Biggs, continued to disappoint and were fourth overall in the standings with just two podium finishes. At Imola the win went to Steinhausen after a superb race in which he left Webster behind by more than 14"! Third place went to Klaffenbock, who still had a slim chance of taking the title from the firm favourite, Webster. Abbott was forced to retire and his fourth place was now under threat from Hanks-Biggs and Martien-van Gils from Holland. The manufacturers' title was wrapped up by Suzuki,

while Swiss firm LCR reigned supreme on the chassis front. After Steve Webster had set pole for the ninth time in nine races and the 36th time in his career, the race saw an undisputed win for Steinhausen-Hopkins, who pulled out a lead of more than seven seconds to take third overall in the championship standings. Second place in the race went to the outgoing champions Abbott-Biggs ahead of Klaffenbach-Parzer who picked up the runner-up slot in the championship. After winning the 2003 title, Webster-Woodhead were never in the hunt for the win and the British pairing were happy to finish fifth overall.

Riders Standing

1	Webster/Woodhead	(GBR)	Suzuki	197
2	Klaffenböck/Parzer	(AUT)	Yamaha	178
3	Steinhausen/Hopkinson	(GER)	Suzuki	161
4	Abbott/Biggs	(GBR)	Yamaha	111
5	Van Gils/Van Gils	(NED)	Suzuki	101
6	Hanks/Biggs	(GBR)	Yamaha	89
7	Philp/Yendell	(GBR)	Suzuki	80
8	Roscher/Hänni	(GER)	Suzuki	76
9	Gatt/Randall	(GBR)	Yamaha	50
10	Skene/Miller	(GBR)	Suzuki	46
11	Gällros/Berglund	(SWE)	Suzuki	43
12	Hauzenberger/Simons	(AUT)	Suzuki	37
13	Morrissey/Harper	(GBR)	Yamaha	37
14	Minguet/Bidault	(FRA)	Suzuki	28
15	Reeves/Reeves	(GBR)	Yamaha	25
16	Doppler/Wagner	(AUT)	Yamaha	22
17	Founds/Long	(GBR)	Yamaha	20
18	Dernoncourt/Lailheugue	(FRA)	Suzuki	15
19	Fleury/Fleury	(NZL)	Yamaha	12
20	Fisher/Long	(GBR)	Yamaha	11
21	Hendry/Wilson	(GBR)	Suzuki	11
22	Le Bail/Chaigneau	(FRA)	Yamaha	10
23	Pedder/Parnell	(GBR)	Yamaha	10
24	Steenbergen/Steenbergen	(NED)	Suzuki	7
25	Lovelock/Holloway	(GBR)	Suzuki	6
26	Cameron/Cox	(GBR)	Suzuki	4
27	Peach/Lawrence	(GBR)	Suzuki	4
28	Stafford/Long	(GBR)	Yamaha	4
29	Woodard/English	(GBR)	Yamaha	3
30	Lindström/Riedel/Riedel	(SWE)	Yamaha	1

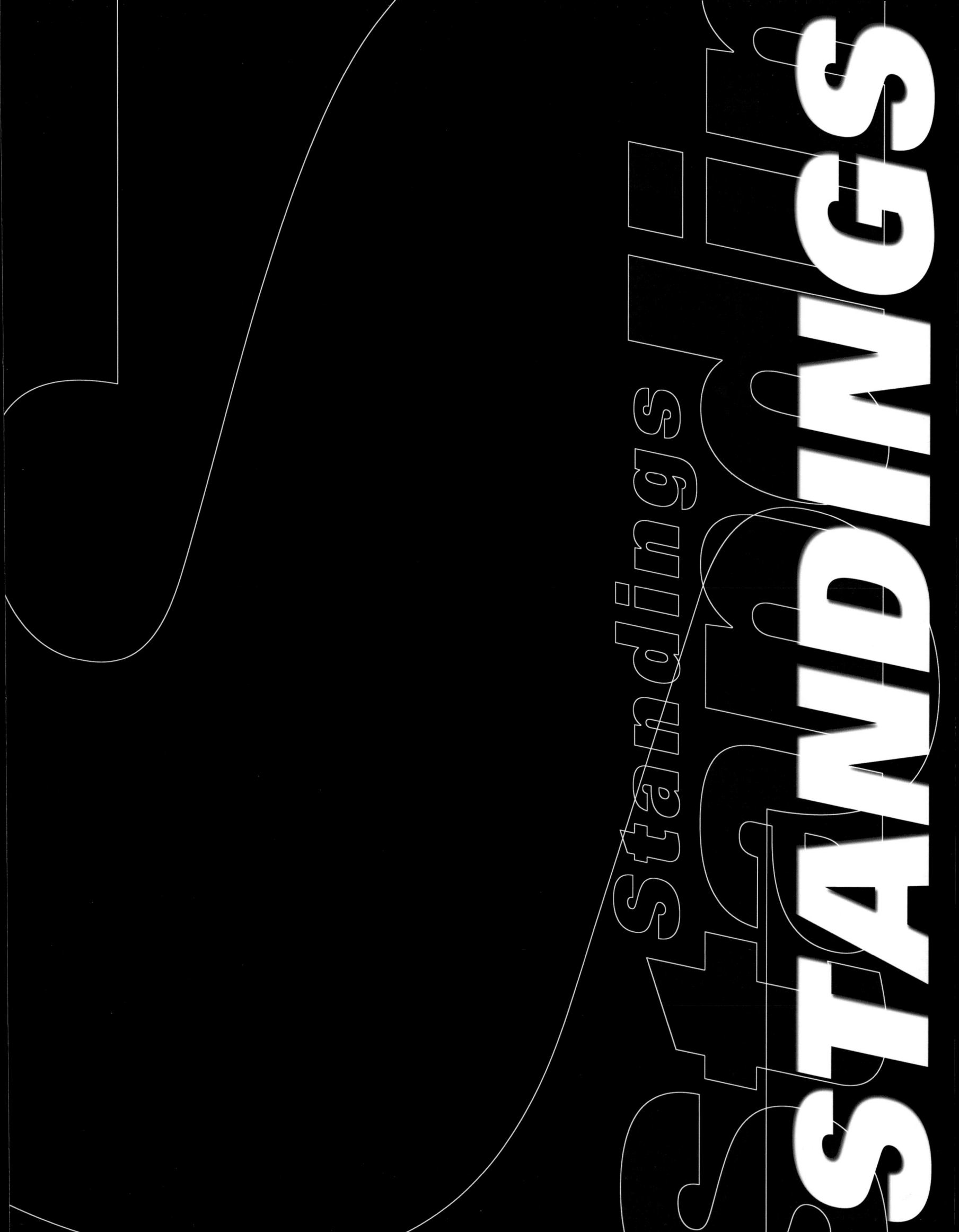

Valencia (ESP) • 02/03/03

Race 1

1	N. HODGSON	GBR	Ducati 999F03	36'56.205
2	R. XAUS	ESP	Ducati 999F03	37'00.905
3	C. WALKER	GBR	Ducati 998F02	37'08.582
4	J. TOSELAND	GBR	Ducati 998F02	37'08.887
5	R. LACONI	FRA	Ducati 998RS	37'20.273
6	S. MARTIN	AUS	Ducati 998RS	37'23.211
7	G.LAVILLA	ESP	Suzuki GSX 1000R	37'35.997
8	L. PEDERCINI	ITA	Ducati 998RS	37'45.867
9	M. BORCIANI	ITA	Ducati 998RS	37'52.405
10	D. GARCIA	ESP	Ducati 998RS	38'02.533
11	I. CLEMENTI	ITA	Kawasaki ZX7RR	38'05.344
12	J. HAYDON	GBR	Foggy FP1	38'05.746
13	N. RUSSO	ITA	Ducati 998RS	38'10.655
14	J. BORJA	ESP	Ducati 998RS	38'10.917
15	S. FUERTES	ESP	Suzuki GSX 1000R	38'19.050
16	M. ISAAC	ESP	Yamaha YZF R1	1 lap

Not Classified:

RET	P. CHILI	ITA	Ducati 998RS	33'23.396
RET	G. BUSSEI	ITA	Yamaha YZF R1	23'13.745
RET	A. GRAMIGNI	ITA	Yamaha YZF R1	23'37.336
RET	S. FOTI	ITA	Ducati 998RS	17'24.078
RET	T. CORSER	AUS	Foggy FP1	14'44.875
RET	W. TORTOROGLIO	ITA	Honda VTR 1000 SP2	15'14.566
RET	M. SANCHINI	ITA	Kawasaki ZX7RR	6'41.626

Race 2

1	N.HODGSON	GBR	Ducati 999F03	36'46.191
2	R. XAUS	ESP	Ducati 999F03	36'48.810
3	J. TOSELAND	GBR	Ducati 998F02	36'59.659
4	C. WALKER	GBR	Ducati 998F02	37'09.617
5	S. MARTIN	AUS	Ducati 998RS	37'22.730
6	G.LAVILLA	ESP	Suzuki GSX 1000R	37'24.785
7	T. CORSER	AUS	Foggy FP1	37'29.160
8	J. BORJA	ESP	Ducati 998RS	37'37.816
9	L. PEDERCINI	ITA	Ducati 998RS	37'39.015
10	M. BORCIANI	ITA	Ducati 998RS	37'40.912
11	G.BUSSEI	ITA	Yamaha YZF R1	37'46.701
12	D. GARCIA	ESP	Ducali 998RS	37'48.305
13	M. SANCHINI	ITA	Kawasaki ZX7RR	37'48.584
14	I. CLEMENTI	ITA	Kawasaki ZX7RR	37'56.076
15	N. RUSSO	ITA	Ducati 998RS	38'03.888
16	W. TORTOROGLIO	ITA	Honda VTR 1000 SP2	38'14.711
17	M. ISAAC	ESP	Yamaha YZF R1	1 lap

Not Classified:

RET	S. FUERTES	ESP	Suzuki GSX 1000R	26'29.904
RET	P. CHILI	ITA	Ducati 998RS	22'12.149
RET	J. HAYDON	GBR	Racing Foggy FP1	15'10.863
RET	R. LACONI	FRA	Ducati 998RS	8'07.142
RET	S. FOTI	ITA	Ducati 998RS	3'46.803
NS	A. GRAMIGNI	ITA	Yamaha YZF R1	

standings

Phillip Island (AUS) • 30/03/03

Race 1

1	N.HODGSON	GBR	Ducati 999F03	34'51.974
2	R. XAUS	ESP	Ducati 999F03	34'59.719
3	G.LAVILLA	ESP	Suzuki GSX 1000R	35'03.454
4	S. MARTIN	AUS	Team Ducati 998RS	35'09.942
5	T. CORSER	AUS	Petronas Foggy FP1	35'10.327
6	R. LACONI	FRA	Ducati 998RS	35'10.621
7	C. WALKER	GBR	Ducati 998F02	35'12.291
8	D. GARCIA	ESP	Ducati 998RS	35'21.705
9	M. BORCIANI	ITA	Ducati 998RS	35'22.087
10	L. PEDERCINI	ITA	Ducati 998RS	35'22.200
11	I. CLEMENTI	ITA	Kawasaki ZX7RR	35'22.504
12	J. BORJA	ESP	Ducati 998RS	35'35.634
13	M. SANCHINI	ITA	Kawasaki ZX7RR	35'39.579
14	G. BUSSEI	ITA	Yamaha YZF R1	35'39.598
15	J. HAYDON	GBR	Petronas Foggy FP1	35'57.685
16	N. RUSSO	ITA	Ducati 998RS	36'21.577
17	J. NORMOYLE	AUS	Suzuki GSX 1000R	1 lap
18	S. CUTTING	AUS	Suzuki GSX 1000R	1 lap
19	A. MAXWELL	AUS	Honda CBR 954	1 lap

Not Classified:

RET	W. TORTOROGLIO	ITA	Honda VTR 1000 SP2	24'25.024
RET	P. CHILI	ITA	Ducati 998RS	6'23.225

Squalified:

	J. TOSELAND	GBR	Ducati 998F02	11'13.202

Race 2

1	N. HODGSON	GBR	Ducati 999F03	34'44.425
2	R. XAUS	ESP	Ducati 999F03	34'44.495
3	P. CHILI	ITA	Ducati 998RS	34'50.733
4	R. LACONI	FRA	Ducati 998RS	34'50.834
5	J. TOSELAND	GBR	Ducati 998F02	34'58.827
6	C. WALKER	GBR	Ducati 998F02	34'58.834
7	G. LAVILLA	ESP	Suzuki GSX 1000R	34'58.851
8	T. CORSER	AUS	Petronas Foggy FP1	35'13.070
9	S. MARTIN	AUS	Ducati 998RS	35'18.519
10	M. BORCIANI	ITA	Ducati 998RS	35'19.233
11	I. CLEMENTI	ITA	Kawasaki ZX7RR	35'19.345
12	M. SANCHINI	ITA	Kawasaki ZX7RR	35'20.092
13	N. RUSSO	ITA	Ducati 998RS	35'20.198
14	L. PEDERCINI	ITA	Ducati 998RS	35'39.844
15	J. BORJA	ESP	Ducati 998RS	35'45.839
16	J. HAYDON	GBR	Petronas Foggy FP1	35'49.662
17	W. TORTOROGLIO	ITA	Honda VTR 1000	36'12.206
18	S. CUTTING	AUS	Suzuki GSX 1000R	1 lap
19	J. NORMOYLE	AUS	Suzuki GSX 1000R	1 lap
20	A. MAXWELL	AUS	Honda CBR 954	1 lap

Not Classified:

RET	D. MESSORI	ITA	Yamaha YZF R1	5'17.671
RET	D. GARCIA	ESP	Ducati 998RS	3'16.145
RET	G. BUSSEI	ITA	Yamaha YZF R1	1'53.209

Sugo (JPN) • 27/04/03

Race 1

1	N. HODGSON	GBR	Ducati 999F03	37'57.829
2	R. LACONI	FRA	Ducati 998RS	38'04.996
3	J. TOSELAND	GBR	Ducati 998F02	38'12.682
4	R. XAUS	ESP	Ducati 999F03	38'26.128
5	G. LAVILLA	ESP	Suzuki GSX-R 1000	38'30.211
6	H. IZUTSU	JPN	Honda VTR 1000SPW	38'30.413
7	L. PEDERCINI	ITA	Ducati 998RS	38'58.444
8	A. WATANABE	JPN	Suzuki GSX-R 1000	38'59.983
9	J. HAYDON	GBR	Petronas Foggy FP1	39'05.261
10	J. BORJA	ESP	Ducati 998RS	39'09.275
11	M. SANCHINI	ITA	Kawasaki ZX7RR	39'15.183
12	G. BUSSEI	ITA	Yamaha YZF R1	39'16.799
13	M. BORCIANI	ITA	Ducati 998RS	39'25.675
14	K. NAKAMURA	JPN	Honda VTR 1000	39'25.877
15	S. MARTIN	AUS	Ducati 998RS	1 lap

Not Classified:

RET	W. TORTOROGLIO	ITA	Honda VTR 1000 SP2	28'39.626
RET	N. NUMATA	JPN	Ducati 996 RS	24'54.179
RET	I. CLEMENTI	ITA	Kawasaki ZX7RR	
RET	T. CORSER	AUS	Petronas Foggy FP1	
RET	C. WALKER	GBR	Ducati 998F02	
RET	P. CHILI	ITA	Ducati 998RS	

Race 2

1	N. HODGSON	GBR	Ducati 999F03	37'56.499
2	G. LAVILLA	ESP	Suzuki GSX-R 1000	37'57.317
3	P. CHILI	ITA	Ducati 998RS	37'57.969
4	R. XAUS	ESP	Ducati 999F03	38'06.969
5	J. TOSELAND	GBR	Ducati 998F02	38'07.632
6	H. IZUTSU	JPN	Honda VTR 1000SPW	38'18.103
7	R. LACONI	FRA	Ducati 998RS	38'18.452
8	I. CLEMENTI	ITA	Kawasaki ZX7RR	38'45.356
9	J. BORJA	ESP	Ducati 998RS	38'58.269
10	M. SANCHINI	ITA	Kawasaki ZX7RR	39'01.788
11	G. BUSSEI	ITA	Yamaha YZF	39'05.824
12	T. CORSER	AUS	Foggy PETRONAS FP1	39'11.783
13	M. BORCIANI	ITA	Ducati 998RS	1 lap
14	K. NAKAMURA	JPN	Honda VTR 1000 SP2	1 lap
15	W. TORTOROGLIO	ITA	Honda VTR 1000 SP2	1 lap

Not Classified:

RET	A. WATANABE	JPN	Suzuki GSX-R 1000	20'31.010
RET	N. NUMATA	JPN	Ducati 996 RS	11'14.048
RET	J. HAYDON	GBR	Foggy PETRONAS FP1	11'23.013
RET	S. MARTIN	AUS	Ducati 998RS	6'27.620
RET	C. WALKER	GBR	Ducati 998F02	3'09.499
RET	L. PEDERCINI	ITA	Ducati 998RS	

standings

Race 1

1	N. HODGSON	GBR	Ducati 999F03	32'38.264
2	R. LACONI	FRA	Ducati 998RS	32'38.616
3	G. LAVILLA	ESP	Suzuki GSX-R 1000	32'38.653
4	J. TOSELAND	GBR	Ducati 998F02	32'38.660
5	P. CHILI	ITA	Ducati 998RS	32'39.881
6	C. WALKER	GBR	Ducati 998F02	33'02.402
7	R. XAUS	ESP	Ducati 999F03	33'09.153
8	M. BORCIANI	ITA	Ducati 998RS	33'09.873
9	S. MARTIN	AUS	Ducati 998RS	33'11.141
10	L. PEDERCINI	ITA	Ducati 998RS	33'14.166
11	A. GRAMIGNI	ITA	Yamaha YZF R1	33'19.964
12	V. IANNUZZO	ITA	Suzuki GSX 1000R	33'24.136
13	T. CORSER	AUS	PETRONAS Foggy FP1	33'32.468
14	M. SANCHINI	ITA	Kawasaki ZX7RR	33'51.670
15	S. FOTI	ITA	Ducati 998RS	34'05.968
16	S. FUERTES	ESP	Suzuki GSX 1000R	34'10.188
17	L. MAURI	ITA	Ducati 996 RS	1 lap
18	M. MASETTI	ITA	Ducati 996 RS	1 lap

Not Classified:

RET	I. CLEMENTI	ITA	Kawasaki ZX7RR	30'39.915
RET	J. HAYDON	GBR	PETRONAS Foggy FP1	27'04.720
RET	G. BUSSEI	ITA	Yamaha YZF R1	27'48.778
RET	W. TORTOROGLIO	ITA	Honda VTR 1000 SP2	3'52.421

Race 2

1	N. HODGSON	GBR	Ducati 999F03	32'41.366
2	G. LAVILLA	ESP	Suzuki GSX-R 1000	32'41.410
3	P. CHILI	ITA	Ducati 998RS	32'42.023
4	R. LACONI	FRA	Ducati 998RS	32'42.364
5	J. TOSELAND	GBR	Ducati 998F02	32'47.745
6	C. WALKER	GBR	Ducati 998F02	33'08.655
7	S. MARTIN	AUS	Ducati 998RS	33'20.951
8	M. BORCIANI	ITA	Ducati 998RS	33'21.186
9	V. IANNUZZO	ITA	Suzuki GSX 1000R	33'21.247
10	L. PEDERCINI	ITA	Ducati 998RS	33'24.772
11	A. GRAMIGNI	ITA	Yamaha YZF R1	33'32.606
12	M. SANCHINI	ITA	Kawasaki ZX7RR	33'38.857
13	G. BUSSEI	ITA	Yamaha YZF R1	33'38.869
14	S. FOTI	ITA	Ducati 998RS	34'12.022
15	W. TORTOROGLIO	ITA	Honda VTR 1000 SP2	34'22.776
16	M. MASETTI	ITA	Ducati 996 RS	34'31.128
17	L. MAURI	ITA	Ducati 996 RS	1 lap

Not Classified:

RET	R. XAUS	ESP	Ducati 999F03	29'08.934
RET	I. CLEMENTI	ITA	Kawasaki ZX7RR	28'49.365
RET	T. CORSER	AUS	PETRONAS Foggy FP1	25'58.710
RET	S. FUERTES	ESP	Suzuki GSX 1000R	26'32.091
RET	J. HAYDON	GBR	PETRONAS Foggy FP1	22'43.098

Oschersleben (GER) • 01/06/03

Race 1

1	N. HODGSON	GBR	Ducati 999F03	41'29.894
2	P. CHILI	ITA	Ducati 998RS	41'30.450
3	J. TOSELAND	GBR	Ducati 998F02	41'42.859
4	R. LACONI	FRA	Ducati 998RS	41'46.524
5	C. WALKER	GBR	Ducati 998F02	41'46.648
6	S. MARTIN	AUS	Ducati 998RS	42'08.036
7	M. BORCIANI	ITA	Ducati 998RS	42'13.390
8	V. IANNUZZO	ITA	Suzuki GSX 1000R	42'15.346
9	L. PEDERCINI	ITA	Ducati 998RS	42'20.048
10	G. BUSSEI	ITA	Yamaha YZF R1	42'21.112
11	M. SANCHINI	ITA	Kawasaki ZX7RR	42'34.247
12	T. CORSER	AUS	Petronas FP1	42'40.537
13	N. RUSSO	ITA	Ducati 998RS	41'34.246
14	S. FOTI	ITA	Ducati 998RS	41'51.203
15	J. MRKYVKA	CZE	Ducati 998RS	42'02.782
16	S. FUERTES	ESP	Suzuki GSX 1000R	42'11.186
17	S. DAG STEINAR	NOR	Yamaha YZF R1	42'43.446

Not Classified:

RET	J. HAYDON	GBR	Petronas FP1	21'34.487
RET	W. TORTOROGLIO	ITA	Honda VTR 1000 SP2	21'41.488
RET	R. XAUS	ESP	Ducati 999F03	13'26.186
RET	J. BORJA	ESP	Ducati 998RS	6'04.225
RET	I. CLEMENTI	ITA	Kawasaki ZX7RR	1'37.105
RET	G. LAVILLA	ESP	Suzuki GSX-R 1000	

Race 2

1	J. TOSELAND	GBR	Ducati 998F02	41'20.103
2	N. HODGSON	GBR	Ducati 999F03	41'27.519
3	C. WALKER	GBR	Ducati 998F02	41'35.417
4	R. LACONI	FRA	Ducati 998RS	41'39.380
5	R. XAUS	ESP	Ducati 999F03	41'44.331
6	S. MARTIN	AUS	Ducati 998RS	42'03.751
7	J. BORJA	ESP	Ducati 998RS	42'06.971
8	V. IANNUZZO	ITA	Suzuki GSX 1000R	42'07.910
9	M. BORCIANI	ITA	Ducati 998RS	42'09.033
10	L. PEDERCINI	ITA	Ducati 998RS	42'22.617
11	P. CHILI	ITA	Ducati 998RS	42'30.497
12	M. SANCHINI	ITA	Kawasaki ZX7RR	42'32.789
13	I. CLEMENTI	ITA	Kawasaki ZX7RR	42'33.122
14	T. CORSER	AUS	Petronas FP1	42'47.490
15	S. FOTI	ITA	Ducati 998RS	1 lap
16	S. FUERTES	ESP	Suzuki GSX 1000R	1 lap
17	J. MRKYVKA	CZE	Ducati 998RS	1 lap
18	W. TORTOROGLIO	ITA	Honda VTR 1000 SP2	1 lap
19	S. DAG STEINAR	NOR	Yamaha YZF R1	1 lap

Not Classified:

RET	G. LAVILLA	ESP	Suzuki GSX-R 1000	24'34.617
RET	N. RUSSO	ITA	Ducati 998RS	24'36.851
RET	G. BUSSEI	ITA	Yamaha YZF R1	15'30.819

Silverstone (GBR) • 15/06/03

Race 1

1	N. HODGSON	GBR	Ducati 999F03	38'24.187
2	J. TOSELAND	GBR	Ducati 998F02	38'24.627
3	R. XAUS	ESP	Ducati 999F03	38'24.786
4	R. LACONI	FRA	Ducati 998RS	38'25.130
5	Y. KAGAYAMA	JPN	Suzuki GSX-R 1000	38'28.966
6	J. REYNOLDS	GBR	Suzuki GSX-R 1000	38'29.272
7	P. CHILI	ITA	Ducati 998RS	38'30.129
8	M. RUTTER	GBR	Ducati 998F02	38'30.558
9	C. WALKER	GBR	Ducati 998F02	38'31.416
10	M. BORCIANI	ITA	Ducati 998RS	38'58.586
11	L. PEDERCINI	ITA	Ducati 998RS	39'03.447
12	G. BUSSEI	ITA	Yamaha YZF R1	39'07.574
13	M. SANCHINI	ITA	Kawasaki ZX7RR	39'09.453
14	I. CLEMENTI	ITA	Kawasaki ZX7RR	39'09.815
15	N. RUSSO	ITA	Ducati 998RS	39'10.575
16	T. CORSER	AUS	Petronas FP1	39'18.553
17	S. FUERTES	ESP	Suzuki GSX-R 1000	39'21.469

Not Classified:

RET	G. LAVILLA	ESP	Suzuki GSX-R 1000	30'45.123
RET	V. IANNUZZO	ITA	Suzuki GSX-R 1000	24'07.423
RET	S. FOTI	ITA	Ducati 998RS	22'09.007
RET	S. EMMETT	GBR	Ducati 998F02	5'50.283
RET	W. TORTOROGLIO	ITA	Honda VTR 1000 SP2	6'14.591
RET	J. BORJA	ESP	Ducati 998RS	2'01.525
RET	S. MARTIN	AUS	Ducati 998RS	2'01.669
NS	D. GARCIA	ESP	Ducati 998RS	

Race 2

1	N. HODGSON	GBR	Ducati 999F03	38'13.944
2	G. LAVILLA	ESP	Suzuki GSX-R 1000	38'14.437
3	R. XAUS	ESP	Ducati 999F03	38'14.597
4	J. TOSELAND	GBR	Ducati 998F02	38'17.379
5	Y. KAGAYAMA	JPN	Suzuki GSX-R 1000	38'18.061
6	R. LACONI	FRA	Ducati 998RS	38'18.164
7	P. CHILI	ITA	Ducati 998RS	38'21.190
8	C. WALKER	GBR	Ducati 998F02	38'25.766
9	M. RUTTER	GBR	Ducati 998F02	38'26.343
10	J. REYNOLDS	GBR	Suzuki GSX-R 1000	38'52.443
11	L. PEDERCINI	ITA	Ducati 998RS	38'58.435
12	G. BUSSEI	ITA	Yamaha YZF R1	39'01.973
13	M. BORCIANI	ITA	Ducati 998RS	39'02.747
14	M. SANCHINI	ITA	Kawasaki ZX7RR	39'02.938
15	V. IANNUZZO	ITA	Suzuki GSX-R 1000	39'03.286
16	I. CLEMENTI	ITA	Kawasaki ZX7RR	39'03.507
17	S. FUERTES	ESP	Suzuki GSX-R 1000	39'26.347
18	N. RUSSO	ITA	Ducati 998R	39'26.879

Not Classified:

RET	S. FOTI	ITA	Ducati 998RS	28'22.045
RET	S. MARTIN	AUS	Ducati 998RS	15'40.613
RET	T. CORSER	AUS	Petronas FP1	12'11.197
RET	J. BORJA	ESP	Ducati 998RS	12'11.508
RET	S. EMMETT	GBR	Ducati 998F02	13'10.493
RET	W. TORTOROGLIO	ITA	Honda VTR 1000	8'14.271
NS	D. GARCIA	ESP	Ducati 998R	

Misano (RSM) • 22/06/03

Race 1

1	R. XAUS	ESP	Ducati 999F03	40'22.423
2	J. TOSELAND	GBR	Ducati 998F02	40'23.183
3	R. LACONI	FRA	Ducati 998RS	40'24.134
4	G. LAVILLA	ESP	Suzuki GSX-R 1000	40'33.356
5	C. WALKER	GBR	Ducati 998F02	40'42.910
6	S. MARTIN	AUS	Ducati 998RS	40'45.657
7	T. CORSER	AUS	Petronas FP1	40'49.506
8	L. PEDERCINI	ITA	Ducati 998RS	40'54.449
9	M. SANCHINI	ITA	Kawasaki ZX7RR	40'59.124
10	I. CLEMENTI	ITA	Kawasaki ZX7RR	41'10.960
11	M. BORCIANI	ITA	Ducati 998RS	41'17.059
12	A. GRAMIGNI	ITA	Yamaha YZF R1	41'19.743
13	P. BLORA	ITA	Ducati 996 RS	41'23.507
14	S. FOTI	ITA	Ducati 998RS	41'32.426
15	S. FUERTES	ESP	Suzuki GSX-R 1000	41'46.846
16	G. ZANNINI	ITA	Ducati 998RS	41'48.884
17	L. PINI	ITA	Suzuki GSX-R 1000	41'56.302

Not Classified:

RET	P. CHILI	ITA	Ducati 998RS	38'46.093
RET	V. IANNUZZO	ITA	Suzuki GSX-R 1000	24'27.507
RET	G. BUSSEI	ITA	Yamaha YZF R1	16'38.104
RET	W. TORTOROGLIO	ITA	Honda VTR 1000 SP2	15'13.600
RET	J. MRKYVKA	CZE	Ducati 998RS	10'14.845
RET	J. BORJA	ESP	Ducati 998RS	4'58.642
RET	N. HODGSON	GBR	Ducati 999F03	1'40.521
RET	N. RUSSO	ITA	Ducati 998RS	1'47.582
RET	C. ZAISER	AUT	Aprilia RSV 1000	

Race 2

1	R. XAUS	ESP	Ducati 999F03	40'17.321
2	N. HODGSON	GBR	Ducati 999F03	40'17.565
3	P. CHILI	ITA	Ducati 998RS	40'24.217
4	R. LACONI	FRA	Ducati 998RS	40'31.135
5	G. LAVILLA	ESP	Suzuki GSX-R 1000	40'34.720
6	L. PEDERCINI	ITA	Ducati 998RS	40'36.666
7	V. IANNUZZO	ITA	Suzuki GSX-R 1000	40'41.972
8	C. WALKER	GBR	Ducati 998F02	40'46.485
9	S. MARTIN	AUS	Ducati 998RS	40'49.631
10	T. CORSER	AUS	Petronas FP1	40'50.837
11	M. SANCHINI	ITA	Kawasaki ZX7RR	41'01.518
12	J. BORJA	ESP	Ducati 998RS	41'09.568
13	I. CLEMENTI	ITA	Kawasaki ZX7RR	41'09.949
14	M. BORCIANI	ITA	Ducati 998RS	41'18.766
15	A. GRAMIGNI	ITA	Yamaha YZF R1	41'19.766
16	S. FUERTES	ESP	Suzuki GSX-R 1000	41'29.049
17	P. BLORA	ITA	Ducati 996 RS	41'34.673
18	G. ZANNINI	ITA	Ducati 998RS	41'47.169
19	L. PINI	ITA	Suzuki GSX-R 1000	41'54.032

Not Classified:

RET	J. TOSELAND	GBR	Ducati 998F02	22'44.224
RET	J. MRKYVKA	CZE	Ducati 998RS	18'39.472
RET	N. RUSSO	ITA	Ducati 998RS	16'35.106
RET	G. BUSSEI	ITA	Yamaha YZF R1	3'24.636
RET	S. FOTI	ITA	Ducati 998RS	3'27.701
RET	W. TORTOROGLIO	ITA	Honda VTR 1000 SP2	1'48.549
NS	C. ZAISER	AUT	Aprilia RSV 1000	
NS	D. GARCIA	ESP	Ducati 998RS	

Laguna Seca (USA) • 13/07/03

Race 1

1	P. CHILI	ITA	Ducati 998RS	40'35.653
2	N. HODGSON	GBR	Ducati 999F03	40'38.721
3	J. TOSELAND	GBR	Ducati 998F02	40'41.725
4	M. MLADIN	AUS	Suzuki GSX-R 1000	1'26.061
5	C. WALKER	GBR	Ducati 998F02	40'47.975
6	A. YATES	USA	Suzuki GSX-R 1000	40'57.258
7	G. BUSSEI	ITA	Ducati 998RS	40'57.544
8	T. CORSER	AUS	Petronas FP1	41'02.721
9	M. SANCHINI	ITA	Kawasaki ZX7RR	41'24.940
10	M. BORCIANI	ITA	Ducati 998RS	41'25.332
11	J. BORJA	ES	Ducati 998RS	41'25.914
12	W. TORTOROGLIO	ITA	Honda VTR 1000 SP2	1 lap
13	L. PEDERSOLI	ITA	Ducati 998RS	1 lap

Not Classified:

RET G. LAVILLA	ESP	Suzuki GSX-R 1000	41'31.702
RET R. LACONI	FRA	Ducati 998RS	32'06.599
RET R. XAUS	ESP	Ducati 999F03	23'12.806
RET S. MARTIN	AUS	Ducati 998RS	15'57.344
RET L. PEDERCINI	ITA	Ducati 998RS	16'11.699
RET D. GARCIA	ESP	Ducati 998RS	16'20.558
RET J. MRKYVKA	CZE	Ducati 998RS	6'02.646
RET J. HAYDON	GBR	Petronas FP1	6'10.050
RET I. CLEMENTI	ITA	Kawasaki ZX7RR	1'38.234
NS E. BOSTROM	USA	Kawasaki 750	1'39.081

Race 2

1	R. XAUS	ESP	Ducati 999F03	40'43.876
2	N. HODGSON	GBR	Ducati 999F03	40'55.441
3	C. WALKER	GBR	Ducati 998F02	40'56.940
4	R. LACONI	FRA	Ducati 998RS	40'59.436
5	G. LAVILLA	ESP	Suzuki GSX-R 1000	41'00.230
6	G. BUSSEI	ITA	Ducati 998RS	41'03.561
7	J. BORJA	ESP	Ducati 998RS	41'17.370
8	M. SANCHINI	ITA	Kawasaki ZX7RR	41'19.440
9	M. BORCIANI	ITA	Ducati 998RS	41'19.735
10	L. PEDERCINI	ITA	Ducati 998RS	41'23.206

Not Classified:

RET I. CLEMENTI	ITA	Kawasaki ZX7RR	39'51.777
RET A. YATES	USA	Suzuki GSX-R 1000	35'07.485
RET J. TOSELAND	GBR	Ducati 998F02	24'47.917
RET L. PEDERSOLI	ITA	Ducati 998RS	26'01.648
RET T. CORSER	AUS	Petronas FP1	20'41.353
RET J. MRKYVKA	CZE	Ducati 998RS	6'08.293
RET J. HAYDON	GBR	Petronas FP1	4'41.993
RET W. TORTOROGLIO	ITA	Honda VTR 1000 SP2	4'41.997
RET D. GARCIA	ESP	Ducati 998RS	3'06.630
RET S. MARTIN	AUS	Ducati 998RS	
RET P. CHILI	ITA	Ducati 998RS	
NS E. BOSTROM	USA	Kawasaki 750	
NS M. MLADIN	AUS	Suzuki GSX-R 1000	

Brands Hatch (EUR) • 27/07/03

Race 1

1	S. BYRNE	GBR	Ducati 998F02	36'25.400
2	N. HODGSON	GBR	Ducati 999F03	36'31.199
3	C. WALKER	GBR	Ducati 998F02	36'31.318
4	R. LACONI	FRA	Ducati 998RS	36'32.208
5	S. EMMETT	GBR	Ducati 998RS	36'35.063
6	J. TOSELAND	GBR	Ducati 998F02	36'35.326
7	G. LAVILLA	ESP	Suzuki GSX-R 1000	36'35.770
8	M. RUTTER	GBR	Ducati 998F02	36'57.865
9	P. CHILI	ITA	Ducati 998RS	36'58.124
10	Y. KAGAYAMA	JPN	Suzuki GSX-R 1000	37'01.618
11	D. ELLISON	GBR	Ducati 996	37'11.198
12	J. BORJA	ESP	Ducati 998RS	37'17.702
13	I. CLEMENTI	ITA	Kawasaki ZX7RR	37'18.641
14	S. MARTIN	AUS	Ducati 998RS	37'19.576
15	M. SANCHINI	ITA	Kawasaki ZX7RR	37'34.934
16	A. GRAMIGNI	ITA	Yamaha YZF R1	37'36.992
17	J. HAYDON	GBR	Petronas FP1	37'55.867
18	G. DE MATTEIS	ITA	Ducati 998RS	1 lap
19	L. PEDERSOLI	ITA	Ducati 998RS	1 lap

Not Classified:

RET T. CORSER	AUS	Petronas FP1	32'43.968
RET R. XAUS	ESP	Ducati 999F03	21'56.859
RET M. BORCIANI	ITA	Ducati 998RS	19'30.532
RET L. HASLAM	GBR	Ducati 998RS	22'57.087
RET J. REYNOLDS	GBR	Suzuki GSX-R 1000	16'03.871
RET S. FUERTES	ESP	Suzuki GSX-R 1000	16'46.695
RET L. PEDERCINI	ITA	Ducati 998RS	13'39.968
RET W. TORTOROGLIO	ITA	Honda VTR 1000	13'58.466
RET N. MEDD	GBR	Ducati 998RS	10'53.460
RET J. MRKYVKA	CZE	Ducati 998RS	4'46.976

Race 2

1	S. BYRNE	GBR	Ducati 998F02	36'25.639
2	J. REYNOLDS	GBR	Suzuki GSX-R 1000	36'26.178
3	J. TOSELAND	GBR	Ducati 998F02	36'28.530
4	R. XAUS	ESP	Ducati 999F03	36'30.501
5	N. HODGSON	GBR	Ducati 999F03	36'31.443
6	G. LAVILLA	ESP	Suzuki GSX-R 1000	36'35.132
7	P. CHILI	ITA	Ducati 998RS	36'41.688
8	R. LACONI	FRA	Ducati 998RS	36'43.410
9	Y. KAGAYAMA	JPN	Suzuki GSX-R 1000	36'54.929
10	L. HASLAM	GBR	Ducati 998RS	36'57.123
11	A. GRAMIGNI	ITA	Yamaha YZF R1	37'28.059
12	D. ELLISON	GBR	Ducati 996	37'28.092
13	I. CLEMENTI	ITA	Kawasaki ZX7RR	37'28.388
14	M. BORCIANI	ITA	Ducati 998RS	37'28.947
15	M. SANCHINI	ITA	Kawasaki ZX7RR	37'33.138
16	L. PEDERCINI	ITA	Ducati 998RS	37'41.859
17	S. FUERTES	ESP	Suzuki GSX-R 1000	1 lap

Not Classified:

RET M. RUTTER	GBR	Ducati 998F02	30'51.109
RET J. BORJA	ESP	Ducati 998RS	25'25.151
RET C. WALKER	GBR	Ducati 998F02	20'29.932
RET N. MEDD	GBR	Ducati 998RS	22'43.699
RET J. MRKYVKA	CZE	Ducati 998RS	14'04.462
RET W. TORTOROGLIO	ITA	Honda VTR 1000 SP2	12'28.801
RET S. MARTIN	AUS	Ducati 998RS	10'36.166
RET L. PEDERSOLI	ITA	Ducati 998RS	10'48.276
RET S. EMMETT	GBR	Ducati 998RS	9'20.406
RET T. CORSER	AUS	Petronas FP1	4'32.659
RET J. HAYDON	GBR	Petronas FP1	3'09.212
RET G. DE MATTEIS	ITA	Ducati 998RS	1'38.823

standings

Assen (NED) • 07/09/03

Race 1

1	R. XAUS	ESP	Ducati 999F03	33'07.249
2	N. HODGSON	GBR	Ducati 999F03	33'07.858
3	P. CHILI	ITA	Ducati 998RS	33'08.084
4	J. TOSELAND	GBR	Ducati 998F02	33'08.311
5	C. WALKER	GBR	Ducati 998F02	33'21.986
6	T. CORSER	AUS	Petronas FP1	33'30.230
7	L. HASLAM	GBR	Ducati 998RS	33'30.367
8	I. CLEMENTI	ITA	Kawasaki ZX7RR	33'30.599
9	S. MARTIN	AUS	Ducati 998RS	33'53.111
10	M. SANCHINI	ITA	Kawasaki ZX7RR	34'01.413
11	A. GRAMIGNI	ITA	Yamaha YZF R1	34'12.396
12	L. PEDERCINI	ITA	Ducati 998RS	34'47.023
13	H. SAIGER	AUT	Yamaha YZF R1	34'58.698
14	G. LIVERANI	ITA	Yamaha YZF R1	34'59.166
15	J. MRKYVKA	CZE	Ducati 998RS	34'59.665
16	R. MENZEN	NED	Suzuki GSX 1000R	1 lap
17	P. MOOIJMAN	NED	Suzuki GSX 1000R	1 lap

Not Classified:

RET	L. PEDERSOLI	ITA	Ducati 998RS	20'13.842
RET	M. BORCIANI	ITA	Ducati 998RS	17'07.259
RET	R. LACONI	FR	Ducati 998RS	27'15.436
RET	G. LAVILLA	ESP	Suzuki GSX-R 1000	8'19.649
RET	J. REYNOLDS	GBR	Suzuki GSX-R 1000	6'17.626
RET	W. TORTOROGLIO	ITA	Honda VTR 1000	6'32.774
RET	S. NEBEL	GER	Suzuki GSX 1000R	6'32.860
RET	J. BORJA	ESP	Ducati 998RS	2'13.668
RET	K. TRUCHSESS	AUT	Yamaha YZF R1	2'19.278
RET	S. FUERTES	ESP	Suzuki GSX-R 1000	2'44.289

Race 2

1	N. HODGSON	GBR	Ducati 999F03	32'57.759
2	R. XAUS	ESP	Ducati 999F03	32'58.225
3	G. LAVILLA	ESP	Suzuki GSX-R 1000	33'05.558
4	R. LACONI	FRA	Ducati 998RS	33'12.643
5	P. CHILI	ITA	Ducati 998RS	33'17.627
6	L. HASLAM	GBR	Ducati 998RS	33'25.756
7	I. CLEMENTI	ITA	Kawasaki ZX7RR	33'36.765
8	C. WALKER	GBR	Ducati 998F02	33'39.327
9	T. CORSER	AUS	Petronas FP1	33'40.914
10	J. REYNOLDS	GBR	Suzuki GSX-R 1000	33'46.642
11	S. MARTIN	AUS	Ducati 998RS	33'55.078
12	M. SANCHINI	ITA	Kawasaki ZX7RR	34'03.967
13	M. BORCIANI	ITA	Ducati 998RS	34'06.246
14	L. PEDERCINI	ITA	Ducati 998RS	34'12.862
15	A. GRAMIGNI	ITA	Yamaha YZF R1	34'24.887
16	J. BORJA	ESP	Ducati 998RS	34'38.743
17	S. NEBEL	GER	Suzuki GSX 1000R	34'46.013
18	R. MENZEN	NED	Suzuki GSX 1000R	34'57.807
19	G. LIVERANI	ITA	Yamaha YZF R1	35'01.307
20	K. TRUCHSESS	AUT	Yamaha YZF R1	35'11.611
21	P. MOOIJMAN	NED	Suzuki GSX 1000R	1 lap

Not Classified:

RET	J. TOSELAND	GBR	Ducati 998F02	29'34.867
RET	L. PEDERSOLI	ITA	Ducati 998RS	30'44.935
RET	H. SAIGER	AUT	Yamaha YZF R1	28'27.285
RET	S. FUERTES	ESP	Suzuki GSX-R 1000	30'04.902
RET	J. MRKYVKA	CZE	Ducati 998RS	

standings

Imola (ITA) • 28/09/03

Race 1

1	R. XAUS	ESP	Ducati 999F03	38'30.586
2	N. HODGSON	GBR	Ducati 999F03	38'33.379
3	R. LACONI	FRA	Ducati 998RS	38'39.364
4	G. LAVILLA	ESP	Suzuki GSX-R 1000	39'02.930
5	P. CHILI	ITA	Ducati 998RS	39'07.968
6	S. MARTIN	AUS	Ducati 998RS	39'10.162
7	T. CORSER	AUS	Petronas FP1	39'21.426
8	M. SANCHINI	ITA	Kawasaki ZX7RR	39'31.202
9	I. CLEMENTI	ITA	Kawasaki ZX7RR	39'31.892
10	M. BORCIANI	ITA	Ducati 998RS	39'40.111
11	J. BORJA	ESP	Ducati 998RS	39'41.430
12	D. GARCIA	ESP	Ducati 998RS	39'51.601
13	A. GRAMIGNI	ITA	Yamaha YZF R1	40'00.561
14	S. FUERTES	ESP	Suzuki GSX-R 1000	40'04.470
15	L. PINI	ITA	Suzuki GSX-R 1000	40'14.600
16	G. ZANNINI	ITA	Ducati 998RS	1 lap
17	H. SAIGER	AUT	Yamaha YZF R1	1 lap
18	W. TORTOROGLIO	ITA	Honda VTR 1000 SP2	1 lap
19	L. PEDERSOLI	ITA	Ducati 998RS	1 lap
20	G. LIVERANI	ITA	Yamaha YZF R1	1 lap
21	S. CONTI	ITA	Suzuki GSX 1000R	1 lap

Not Classified:

RET	L. PEDERCINI	ITA	Ducati 998RS	24'15.750
RET	L. MAURI	ITA	Ducati 998RS	25'20.522
RET	C. WALKER	GBR	Ducati 998F02	20'20.144
RET	J. HAYDON	GBR	Petronas FP1	10'12.892
RET	J. TOSELAND	GBR	Ducati 998F02	1'57.502
RET	J. MRKYVKA	CZE	Ducati 998RS	2'07.496

Race 2

1	R. XAUS	ESP	Ducati 999F03	38'29.867
2	R. LACONI	FRA	Ducati 998RS	38'41.905
3	G. LAVILLA	ESP	Suzuki GSX-R 1000	38'45.608
4	N. HODGSON	GBR	Ducati 999F03	38'54.713
5	C. WALKER	GBR	Ducati 998F02	38'55.819
6	L. PEDERCINI	ITA	Ducati 998RS	39'21.645
7	T. CORSER	AUS	Petronas FP1	39'25.449
8	M. SANCHINI	ITA	Kawasaki ZX7RR	39'30.726
9	J. BORJA	ESP	Ducati 998RS	39'33.291
10	D. GARCIA	ESP	Ducati 998RS	39'47.791
11	M. BORCIANI	ITA	Ducati 998RS	40'01.674
12	A. GRAMIGNI	ITA	Yamaha YZF R1	40'04.579
13	S. FUERTES	ESP	Suzuki GSX-R 1000	40'13.459
14	H. SAIGER	AUT	Yamaha YZF R1	1 lap
15	L. PINI	ITA	Suzuki GSX-R 1000	1 lap
16	W. TORTOROGLIO	ITA	Honda VTR 1000 SP2	1 lap
17	S. CONTI	ITA	Suzuki GSX 1000R	1 lap

Not Classified:

RET	J. TOSELAND	GBR	Ducati 998F02	27'37.921
RET	G. LIVERANI	ITA	Yamaha YZF R1	27'33.206
RET	P. CHILI	ITA	Ducati 998RS	22'48.158
RET	G. ZANNINI	ITA	Ducati 998RS	21'23.573
RET	L. MAURI	ITA	Ducati 998RS	17'25.367
RET	I. CLEMENTI	ITA	Kawasaki ZX7RR	13'11.401
RET	L. PEDERSOLI	ITA	Ducati 998RS	11'54.185
RET	J. HAYDON	GBR	Petronas FP1	10'00.073
RET	J. MRKYVKA	CZE	Ducati 998RS	2'11.605
RET	S. MARTIN	AUS	Ducati 998RS	2'23.762

Magny-Cours (FRA) • 19/10/03

Race 1

1	N. HODGSON	GBR	Ducati 999F03	39'03.738
2	R. XAUS	ESP	Ducati 999F03	39'04.086
3	C. WALKER	GBR	Ducati 998F02	39'17.449
4	G. LAVILLA	ESP	Suzuki GSX-R 1000	39'17.688
5	J. TOSELAND	GBR	Ducati 998F02	39'25.218
6	R. LACONI	FRA	Ducati 998RS	39'36.158
7	S. MARTIN	AUS	Ducati 998RS	39'44.836
8	T. CORSER	AUS	Petronas FP1	39'44.942
9	J. BORJA	ESP	Ducati 998RS	40'22.475
10	M. SANCHINI	ITA	Kawasaki ZX7RR	40'34.055
11	S. FUERTES	ESP	Suzuki GSX-R 1000	40'50.272
12	C. ZAISER	AUT	Suzuki GSX 1000R	40'51.892
13	B. STEY	FRA	Honda VTR 1000 SP2	1 lap
14	F. PROTAT	FRA	Yamaha YZF R1	1 lap
15	H. SAIGER	AUT	Yamaha YZF R1	1 lap

Not Classified:

RET	P. CHILI	ITA	Ducati 998RS	34'28.494
RET	M. BORCIANI	ITA	Ducati 998RS	33'19.921
RET	A. GRAMIGNI	ITA	Yamaha YZF R1	32'07.039
RET	L. HASLAM	GBR	Ducati 998RS	15'37.383
RET	L. PEDERCINI	ITA	Ducati 998RS	3'31.578
RET	D. GARCIA	ESP	Ducati 998RS	3'56.257
RET	S. GIMBERT	FRA	Suzuki GSX-R 1000	2'09.626
RET	I. CLEMENTI	ITA	Kawasaki ZX7RR	
RET	J. HAYDON	GBR	Petronas FP1	

Race 2

1	R. XAUS	ESP	Ducati 999F03	39'02.330
2	J. TOSELAND	GBR	Ducati 998F02	39'12.765
3	C. WALKER	GBR	Ducati 998F02	39'12.912
4	G. LAVILLA	ESP	Suzuki GSX-R 1000	39'24.583
5	S. MARTIN	AUS	Ducati 998RS	39'37.894
6	L. HASLAM	GBR	Ducati 998RS	39'38.195
7	J. BORJA	ESP	Ducati 998RS	39'59.049
8	S. GIMBERT	FRA	Suzuki GSX-R 1000	40'03.143
9	I. CLEMENTI	ITA	Kawasaki ZX7RR	40'04.637
10	M. SANCHINI	ITA	Kawasaki ZX7RR	40'05.786
11	L. PEDERCINI	ITA	Ducati 998RS	40'35.867
12	A. GRAMIGNI	ITA	Yamaha YZF R1	40'43.564
13	B. STEY	FRA	Honda VTR 1000 SP2	1 lap
14	M. BORCIANI	ITA	Ducati 998RS	1 lap
15	F. PROTAT	FRA	Yamaha YZF R1	1 lap
16	R. LACONI	FRA	Ducati 998RS	1 lap
17	H. SAIGER	AUT	Yamaha YZF R1	1 lap

Not Classified:

RET	N. HODGSON	GBR	Ducati 999F03	33'54.830
RET	S. FUERTES	ESP	Suzuki GSX-R 1000	36'01.562
RET	P. CHILI	ITA	Ducati 998RS	6'51.694
RET	J. HAYDON	GBR	Petronas FP1	7'04.456
RET	D. GARCIA	ESP	Ducati 998RS	7'34.580
RET	C. ZAISER	AUT	Suzuki GSX 1000R	
RET	T. CORSER	AUS	Petronas FP1	